Catherine Atkinson has a degree in Food and Nutrition BSc (Hons). She has been Deputy Cookery Editor on *Woman's Weekly* magazine and later Cookery Editor of *Home*. Catherine is now a full-time writer and food consultant to various lifestyle and health magazines and has written more than sixty cookbooks. She specialises in baking and her recent published books include *Brilliant Breadmaking in Your Bread Machine*, *Muffins Galore* and *The Vegan Dairy*.

ALSO BY CATHERINE ATKINSON

Muffins Galore
Brilliant Breadmaking in Your Bread Machine
How to Make Your Own Cordials and Syrups
How to Make Perfect Panini
Power Blends and Smoothies
Fermenting Food for Healthy Eating
Cooking with Your Instant Pot
The Vegan Dairy
The Healthy Fibre-rich Cookbook

Baking it Vegan

Easy Recipes for Your Favourite
Cakes and Bakes

Catherine Atkinson

ROBINSON

ROBINSON

First published in Great Britain in 2022 by Robinson

10 9 8 7 6 5 4 3 2 1

A CIP catalogue record for this book is available from the British Library.

ISBN: 978-1-47214-680-9

Typeset by Basement Press, Glaisdale
Printed and bound in Great Britain by Clays Ltd, Elcograf S.p.A.

Papers used by Robinson are from well-managed forests and other responsible sources.

MIX
Paper from
responsible sources
FSC® C104740

Robinson
An imprint of
Little, Brown Book Group
Carmelite House
50 Victoria Embankment
London EC4Y 0DZ

An Hachette UK Company
www.hachette.co.uk

www.littlebrown.co.uk

How To Books are published by Robinson, an imprint of Little, Brown Book Group. We welcome proposals from authors who have first-hand experience of their subjects. Please set out the aims of your book, its target market and its suggested contents in an email to howtobooks@littlebrown.co.uk

Contents

Contents

INTRODUCTION

Whether you are a full-time vegan, cooking for someone who is, or simply choosing to cut down on animal products whenever possible, there's no need to miss out on cakes and bakes. All manner of classic baking recipes have been transformed into delicious vegan-friendly versions, from a beautiful risen Victoria Sponge Cake to decadent Millionaire's Shortbread and tangy Lemon Meringue Pie, all bakes which are traditionally made with butter and eggs.

Vegans eat a wide range of foods but exclude all animal products, including eggs, dairy and any foods that contain ingredients from an animal source. Although many think of veganism as new trend, people around the world have been choosing to eat a vegan diet for thousands of years. It is, however, increasingly common to live in a household where at least one person is a vegan and the number of people identifying as vegan in the UK has more than trebled in the last five years.

As interest in vegan food has grown, the availability of dairy and egg alternatives has soared and plant-based ingredients are much easier to find, with most supermarkets having a section dedicated to vegan products. Consumer demand continues to increase from both vegans and those who are intolerant to dairy foods and egg products.

The transition from traditional baking using dairy products and eggs to using vegan alternatives may seem daunting at first, but vegan baking is surprisingly simple. This book outlines many of the non-dairy ingredients and egg alternatives that are key to a vegan pantry. It covers ways to replicate the various properties of eggs in baking, whether for binding mixtures together or to help a bake aerate or make it rise, and you'll discover how some alternatives to eggs and dairy, such as plant milks, can easily be made at home. Rather than viewing a vegan diet as one that limits what you can eat, think of it as a means of experimenting and trying different kinds of exciting foods.

The aim here is not just to recreate traditional bakes but to make vegan versions that taste fantastic. One of the biggest advantages of home baking is choice and knowing exactly what has gone into your bakes. You have complete control of the ingredients and can make sure that each and every one is vegan. Whether you opt for local sustainable products, organic or fair-trade ingredients is entirely your choice. Turn to the recipes where you'll find over 75 delicious cakes, cookies, pastries and breads; vegans need never miss out again.

A BALANCED VEGAN DIET

Vegan cakes, cookies and pastries are – like traditional bakes – an indulgence to be enjoyed in moderation. While you'll find a number of 'healthier' bakes in the following chapters, the aim of this book is not to produce health-food recipes but to create vegan bakes that are every bit as delicious as their non-vegan counterparts.

Many of the baking swaps you will make as a vegan may be naturally healthier, as eggs and dairy are a source of saturated fat, but this isn't an excuse to overindulge. Be aware that some vegan products such as plant butter contains only slightly less saturated fat than dairy butter. In many recipes, particularly those for cakes, oil is used instead of hard fats. Easy to measure and quicker to mix, it produces excellent results in vegan bakes. Your choice may be a mild oil such as sunflower or blended vegetable oil, but I prefer to bake with rapeseed oil as its rich golden colour and mild nutty flavour enhances many bakes. It has one of the lowest levels of saturated fat of any oil, is high in beneficial monounsaturated fat and a good source of omegas 3 and 6. Produced from the bright yellow rapeseed plant grown all over the UK, it also has a low carbon footprint. Choose a mild-flavoured rapeseed oil for baking, rather than cold-pressed oil which has a stronger taste that will be too distinctive in some bakes.

Plenty of protein

While no sane nutritionist would suggest you make cakes and bakes to provide protein in your diet, they can contribute to your overall intake. Protein is vital for the maintenance and repair of every cell in the body and for producing hormones and antibodies. Made up of amino acids, nine of these are essential as the body cannot make them from food. There are only a few vegan foods which contain all nine and these include soya and products made from them. For this reason, many of the recipes here suggest using unsweetened soya milk, which has one of the highest protein contents of all plant milks (3.3g protein per 100ml/3½fl oz). Tofu is another soya product which is high in protein (8g per 100g/3½oz) and makes a great egg substitute (page 14) in some bakes. Nuts and seeds are also useful protein-rich ingredients which add flavour and texture to many vegan bakes. You may also want to consider using flours such as chickpea flour, besan (gram) flour or quinoa flour in some bakes to boost the protein content.

Must-have minerals

Needed for muscles, bones and teeth and for blood oxygenation and coagulation, there are five minerals which typically come from animal products and for which vegans need to find alternative sources in their diet. These are iron, calcium, selenium, zinc and iodine.

Iron

Found in all cells, iron is a component of hemoglobin needed by red blood cells to carry oxygen around the body. One nutritional advantage of being vegan is that you avoid the casein found in dairy foods, which inhibits iron absorption. Good vegan sources of iron include beans, tofu, cashew nuts, flax (linseed), dried fruit (especially dates and dried apricots) and quinoa including quinoa flour.

Calcium

Our bodies contain over 1kg of this mineral; it's needed for the formation and continuing strength of bones and teeth. There are plenty of vegan foods that are rich in calcium, such as soya products (milk, yogurt and tofu), fruit (including dried apricots), nuts and seeds (including products such as tahini).

Selenium

This micromineral is an antioxidant which helps protects the body from the damaging effect of free radicals and is also important for the thyroid gland and immune system. Brazil nuts are the best vegan source; just one a day will provide you with enough selenium.

Zinc

Crucial during growth and reproduction, zinc also plays a role in supporting the immune system. Vegans can get enough zinc from soya beans and their products, and nuts (especially Brazil nuts and seeds).

Iodine

Necessary for the body to make thyroid hormones, which keep cells healthy and help control metabolic rate. Good sources for vegans are cranberries and strawberries. It is also possible to buy salt fortified with iodine.

Vital vitamins

Vitamins are a group of substances needed in minute quantities for cell function and growth. For the most part, vegans can get all the necessary vitamins they need from food in a well-balanced diet. There are only two that vegans need to take extra steps to include. These are vitamins B12 and D.

Vitamin B12

Vital for producing oxygen-carrying red blood cells, for supporting the nervous system, for the manufacturing of DNA and to process fats and carbohydrates. It is only found naturally in animal products, so vegans need to either take a supplement or buy plant milks and products to which it has been added. Nutritional yeast is sold in small tubes of golden-coloured flakes and gives a cheesy kick to many savoury bakes (you'll find it as an optional addition in some of the recipes in this book). It is also high in protein (50g/1¾oz per 100g/3½oz). Buy a version that is fortified with vitamin B12; many also have folic acid and zinc as well.

Vitamin D

Needed for the absorption of calcium and phosphorus, vitamin D is a family of nutrients. D3 (cholecalciferol) is found in a small number of animal and fish products, whereas D2 (ergocalciferol) can be sourced from vegan foods such as mushrooms grown in UV light. D3 is more effective than D2 at raising blood levels of vitamin D and can also be obtained through exposure of bare skin to sunlight once or twice a day during the summer months without sunscreen (taking care not to burn). It is now recommended that vegans (and non-vegans) take a supplement of vitamin D3 during the winter months.

ALL ABOUT VEGAN MILKS

When it comes to dairy-free cooking, what plant-based milk you choose will depend on personal preference. If you are also using plant milks for pouring over breakfast cereals, making smoothies or adding to hot drinks, you may find it's worth keeping more than one type in the fridge; a rich and creamy nut or seed milk, ideal for dessert-type baking, adding creaminess to fillings and frostings, and a more economical grain milk such as soya or oat milk for plainer bakes. All the recipes in this book have been tested with unsweetened plant milk, so if you only have sweetened milk in your fridge, reduce the sugar in recipes by a tiny amount.

Shop-bought cartons of plant milk are convenient, but they often contain added thickeners and preservatives. If you have the time and inclination you may want to make your own; generally, homemade milks work out a lot less expensive than shop-bought. If you are using plant milks solely for baking, providing you have a powerful blender you can use nut and seed milks unstrained.

NUT AND SEED MILKS

There are a huge amount of nut and seed milks available in the supermarket. The most popular is almond milk, but you can also find hazelnut, cashew nut and hemp seed milk. These may be made with raw or roasted nuts or seeds, sweetened or unsweetened. In health food and specialist vegan food shops you may also find more unusual milks including peanut (groundnut), Brazil nut and walnut milk.

How to make nut and seed milks

Almond and hazelnut milks work well in delicate sponges and mild-flavoured bakes. They have an affinity with many fruits and are also good with both chocolate and coffee. Peanut milk is an inexpensive alternative and works well in more highly flavoured cakes and cookies, particularly spicy ones, where its somewhat distinctive taste enhances rather than dominates. Because seeds are high in fat, they produce wonderfully rich and creamy milks. They also have a good protein, vitamin and mineral content. Simple and inexpensive to make, sunflower seed milk is a versatile seed milk in baking as it has a very subtle nutty flavour and pale creamy colour.

MAKES ABOUT 750ML/1¼ PINTS

175g/6oz raw unsalted blanched almonds, lightly roasted, unsalted skinned hazelnuts or raw or lightly roasted unsalted skinned peanuts or sunflower and/or pumpkin seeds
750ml/1¼ pints water, preferably filtered, plus soaking water

1 Put the nuts or seeds in a large glass, ceramic or stainless-steel bowl. Pour over enough cold water to cover by about 3cm

(1¼in) and leave to soak at room temperature for at least 8 hours or for up to 24 hours in the fridge.

2   Drain and rinse the nuts or seeds, then tip them into a blender and add about 250ml/8½fl oz of the water. Pulse a few times to chop, then blend for 2–3 minutes, or until the mixture is smooth.

3   Pour the mixture through a nut bag or a sieve lined with a layer of muslin into a bowl or jug. Leave to drain, then return the pulp to the blender, add a further 250ml/8½fl oz water and blend again. Drain as before.

4   Pour the remaining water over the pulp. Leave to drain, then gather up the bag or corners of the muslin and squeeze out the last few drops of the milk. Store in glass bottles or in a covered jug in the fridge. Nut milks will keep for up to 4 days, seed milks for 2–3 days. Stir before using.

BEAN AND GRAIN MILKS

A range of healthy plants milks can be made from beans such as soya, pulses such as split peas, and grains such as oats, rice and hemp. Many commercial varieties are fortified with calcium and vitamins such as B12, which is especially useful for those following a vegan diet.

Soya milk – Soya beans (known as edamame beans when fresh) are the basis of soya milk as well as other vegan products such as tofu and miso. Soya milk is excellent for baking, particularly when it is acting as an egg replacer as it has one of the highest protein contents of plant milks. In addition, many supermarkets sell 'economy' brands of unsweetened soya milk. Although most soya beans are imported, some soya milk manufacturers source soya beans grown in the UK. Soya milk can be a problem for anyone who has a thyroid condition as it can interfere with the absorption of medication, so you should make sure that you don't consume soya milk until at least 4 hours after taking medication.

Pea milk – This thick and creamy milk with a mild flavour is made from yellow split peas. High in protein (it contains around eight times as much as shop-bought almond milk and is slightly higher in protein than soya milk), it is also rich in calcium and iron. During manufacture the pea protein is separated from the starch and fibre and blended with water and a little oil. Excellent for vegan baking, pea milk is good from an environmental perspective as peas require much less water for growing than nuts, especially almonds. Unfortunately, it is impossible to replicate the manufacturing process to make your own.

Rice milk – This has a neutral flavour and is useful in baking where a delicately flavoured milk such as hazelnut milk wouldn't enhance the bake or a strongly-flavoured milk would be overpowering. It contains less protein than nut and seed milk, so is less suitable for cakes which rely on a higher-protein milk to work as an egg replacer.

Oat milk – A good option for those who are intolerant to soya, oats contain beta-glucan, a soluble fibre that can help reduce cholesterol. It has less protein and fat than nut milks and is easy and inexpensive to make, but commercial varieties have the benefit of fortification with calcium and vitamin B12.

How to make soya milk

Although it is one of the most time-consuming plant milks to make, if you use or drink soya milk regularly it can be worthwhile as it will cost a fraction of shop-bought. It will keep for up to 4 days so you may want to double the quantity. While most soya beans are imported from China, you can buy soya beans which are grown in the UK.

MAKES ABOUT 1 LITRE/34FL OZ

100g/3½oz dried soya beans, preferably organic
1 litre/34fl oz water, preferably filtered, plus extra for soaking

1   Put the soya beans in a large glass, ceramic or stainless-steel bowl. Pour over enough cold water to cover by about 3cm (1¼in) and leave to soak in the fridge for at least 12 hours or for up to 24 hours in the fridge.

2   Drain the beans and squeeze each one out of its skin; this should be quick and easy after soaking. Discard the skins and rinse the beans.

3   Put the beans in a blender with 600ml/1 pint of the water. Blend until very smooth, then pour the mixture through a nut bag or a sieve lined with a layer of muslin into a saucepan. Leave to drain, then return the pulp to the blender, add a further 200ml/7fl oz of water and blend again. Drain as before.

4   Pour the remaining water over the pulp. Leave to drain, then gather up the bag or corners of the muslin and squeeze out the last few drops of the milk.

5   Bring the soya milk to the boil, reduce the heat, half-cover with a lid and simmer for 15 minutes, skimming off any foam. Turn off the heat and leave to cool. Store in glass bottles or in a covered jug in the fridge for up to 4 days. Shake or stir before using.

How to make oat milk

Oat milk is also good for baking as the flavour is mild and it naturally has a slightly sweet flavour. It will separate quickly unless you add an emulsifier such as lecithin, but you can of course simply give it a good stir before using.

MAKES ABOUT 750ML/1¼ PINTS

100g/3½oz rolled (porridge) oats
750ml/1¼ pints water, preferably filtered, plus extra for
   soaking
a pinch of salt
1 tbsp powdered lecithin (optional)

1   Put the oats in a large glass, ceramic or stainless-steel bowl. Pour over enough cold water to cover by about 3cm (1¼in)

and leave to soak for 15 minutes. Drain and rinse the oats under cold running water (this is important or the milk will have a slimy texture). Drain well.

2 Put the oats, about 600ml/1 pint of the water and the salt in a blender and leave to soak for 10 minutes. Blend for 2–3 minutes until smooth, then pour the mixture through a nut bag or a sieve lined with a layer of muslin over a bowl. Leave to drain.

3 Pour the rest of the water over the pulp and drain again. Gently stir the mixture to help the milk through and press down with the back of the spoon, but do not squeeze.

4 If using emulsifier, return the milk to the clean blender, add the lecithin and blend for a minute. Store in glass bottles or in a covered jug in the fridge for up to 5 days. Shake or stir before using.

TIP
A natural product, lecithin is used by all the cells in the body; it breaks down into choline, which plays an important role in fat metabolism. This creamy-coloured powder sold in small tubs is made from soya beans; it acts as a thickener and emulsifier, helping to prevent the milk from separating, and will lengthen the keeping qualities of plant milk by a day or two.

COCONUT MILK AND CREAM

Coconut milk is usually bought in tins, each brand being slightly different with a varying fat content. Coconut cream is the thick creamy part of coconut milk that rises to the top of the tin, separating out from the more watery milk. You can spoon it off to make coconut cream filling or topping (page 21) or you can shake the tin really well before opening (or whisk together the contents afterwards). It is also sold on its own in small cartons and tins. You can also buy reduced-fat coconut milk, which contains a third less fat than its full-fat counterpart. Coconut milk is also available in powdered form in sachets which can be reconstituted with water. This is very convenient if you only want a small amount of coconut milk for a specific bake.

Dairy evaporated milk and condensed milk can be replaced with evaporated coconut milk and condensed coconut milk. They have a mild coconut taste but this will be barely noticeable when combined with other ingredients.

Coconut 'drink' comes in cartons and you'll find it next to other plant milks in the chiller cabinet and in the supermarket aisle with other long-life milks. Generally it is intended for serving with cereal, or for hot drinks and smoothie making, but it can also be used for baking. Most brands contain around 5% coconut milk and are bulked out with water, rice, stabilisers, thickeners and coconut flavourings. Make sure that you use the product specified in the individual recipe as coconut 'milk' and coconut 'drink' are very different.

VEGAN BAKING INGREDIENTS

There are a small number of useful 'ingredients' that you'll find mentioned in the recipes throughout this book that you can easily make yourself.

Oat flour

A nutritious whole grain flour, oat flour is made from ground rolled oats. With a mild, slightly nutty flavour and sweet taste, it is higher in protein than wheat flours. While oat flour can be purchased ready-made, it is really simple to make yourself. Put the required amount of oats (old-fashioned 'jumbo' oats are best) in a blender or food processor and blitz for 20–30 seconds until ground to a fine powder. It's best to make and use it 'fresh', but once ground, any that you don't need for immediate use can be stored in an airtight container for up to 2 months. Oats are naturally gluten-free but if you are baking for a coeliac or someone with a wheat allergy, make sure you use certified gluten-free oats, as oats can be cross-contaminated by grains grown nearby or in factories when they are processed.

Nut flour

If you make your own nut milk such as almond or cashew nut milk, you can make a flour from the leftover pulp. This will be much lower in fat and flavour than ground nuts, as most of the fats will be in the nut milk you've made, but they can be a useful addition in small quantities to some recipes. Spread the pulp thinly over a baking sheet lined with non-stick baking paper and bake in an oven at 110°C/fan oven 90°C/gas ¼. Bake for 15 minutes, then stir to break up any lumps and bake for a further 10–15 minutes until dry (you can turn the oven off for the last 5 minutes). Remove and leave to cool, then blitz in a food processor to a fine flour. Store in an airtight container for up to 3 weeks or in the freezer for up to 4 months.

Nut butter

If you have a powerful food processor, it is easy to make your own nut butter. Put 175g/6oz unsalted roasted nuts in a food processor and blend until finely chopped. Drizzle 1 tablespoon of groundnut, rapeseed or sunflower oil over the top and blend until the mixture comes together in a clumpy paste. Stop and scrape down the sides of the food processor and continue processing for 2–3 minutes. At first the nut butter will get thicker, but it should gradually become creamier. Take care not to overheat your machine – stop for a few minutes if necessary, then process again.

Apple puree

Often used as an egg substitute (page 14) or as a means to reduce the fat content in recipes, apple puree is easy to make at home and has the advantage that you can control the sugar content (most shop-bought jars of puree are sweetened with sugar and may also contain other additives). Eating apples are best as they are naturally sweet. Quarter, peel and chop the required amount of apples and put in a pan with 2 tablespoons of water or apple juice. Cover and simmer gently for 15 minutes, or until very soft. Allow to cool, then puree with a hand-held stick blender or in a food processor. Store in the fridge for up to 3 days or freeze in portions. 450g/1lb eating apples (4 average-sized) will yield about 300g/10½oz apple puree.

EGG SUBSTITUTES

When it comes to vegan baking, it is relatively simple to find substitutes for ingredients such as dairy milk, creams and soft cheeses, but finding a replacement for eggs can be more challenging. Eggs play a huge role in baking: for binding ingredients and providing structure; for rising, as eggs trap pockets of air when beaten which expand during baking; for giving bakes a good colour and making them crisper.

Aquafaba

The name for this unpromising-looking liquid translates as 'water bean'. It is a brilliant aid for the vegan baker and can be used as a binder or emulsifier but is most noted for its ability to be whisked into a thick frothy mixture just like egg whites. It can be purchased in 200ml/7fl oz cartons, or you can use the liquid drained from a tin of chickpeas. It is freezable, so if you want to make a large batch, cook chickpeas with just enough water to cover them. Use 3 tablespoons of aquafaba to replace 1 whole egg, 2 tablespoons for 1 egg white and 1 tablespoon to replace 1 egg yolk.

Examples: Classic Carrot Cake (page 22), Whoopie Pies (page 106), Lemon Meringue Pie (page 162), French Macarons (page 130), Ginger Oatmeal Cookies (page 120), Pandoro (page 174).

Flax (linseed) and chia seeds

When ground into flour or used in whole form, flax and chia seeds help bind other ingredients and help prevent bakes crumbling.

High in protein and omega-3 fatty acids, the outer layer of the seeds is a mucilage, a sticky layer which when combined with liquid makes a jelly-like emulsion. You can buy ready-ground flax seeds or grind your own to a fine powder using a pestle and mortar or coffee grinder. Chia seeds can also be ground if you don't want large seeds in the finished bake and white chia seeds are available for light-coloured bakes. For the equivalent of 1 egg for binding, use 1 tablespoon of seeds plus 3 tablespoons of water; for raising use 1 tablespoon of seeds plus 3 tablespoons of water and add ¼ teaspoon of baking powder to the dry ingredients. To substitute 1 egg yolk, use 1 tablespoon of seeds plus 2 tablespoons of water. Only use flax and chia seeds as an egg replacer in recipes that need no more than 2 eggs (recipes which traditionally need 3 or more eggs are less successful with egg replacer).

Examples: Citrus Polenta Cake (page 56), Dark Chocolate and Walnut Brownies (page 104).

Silken tofu

Tofu has a very mild flavour that virtually disappears in bakes while adding a protein and calcium boost, which is good news for vegans. Made from the curds of soya milk and sold in a tetrapak block, 'silken' tofu has a very light set and can easily be pureed and used in place of egg and dairy cream/milk mixtures. Use 65g/2½oz silken tofu per egg.

Examples: Creamy Spinach Quiche (page 142), Pumpkin Pie (page 148), Blackcurrant Cheesecake (page 156).

Fruit and vegetable purees

Adding pureed or mashed fruit such as apples and bananas or vegetables such as pumpkin, butternut squash and sweet potato helps bind mixtures together as well as adding sweetness. Packed with vitamins and fibre, finely chopped or pureed dried prunes and dates (blended with liquid such as water or plant milk) provide an alternative to eggs and allow you to reduce the refined sugar and fat content.

For the equivalent of 1 egg use 1 medium mashed banana or 65g/2½oz pureed cooked apples, pumpkin, squash or sweet potato or dates/prunes.

Examples: Bermuda Banana Bread (page 74), Apple and Cranberry Loaf (page 40), Spiced Butternut Squash Teabread page 78), Sweet Potato and Herb Muffins (page 100), Almond Biscotti (page 132).

Chickpea or besan (gram) flour
Also known as garbanzo bean flour or chana flour, this pale brown flour is high in protein and can be used to both bind and help aerate bakes. To replace 1 egg, blend 3 tablespoons of chickpea flour with 3 tablespoons of plant milk until smooth.

Examples: Blueberry Muffins (page 94), Roasted Vegetable Stromboli (page 178).

Bicarbonate of soda and vinegar
Bicarbonate of soda reacts with vinegar to make lots of foamy bubbles that when combined with a liquid such as plant milk can produce light cakes and aerated bakes. Use a mild-flavoured vinegar such as cider vinegar or an acid such as lemon juice. Generally, the bicarbonate of soda is mixed into the dry ingredients and the vinegar or lemon juice blended with the liquid. Use 1 teaspoon each of bicarbonate of soda and 1 teaspoon vinegar or lemon juice plus an extra 3 tablespoons of plant milk or liquid to replace 1 egg.

Examples: Light Fruit Cake (page 26), Chocolate Hazelnut Cupcakes (page 88), Mushroom and Pine Nut Muffins (page 98).

Vegan yogurt and buttermilk and bicarbonate of soda
To make vegan 'buttermilk' put 1 tablespoon of lemon juice or apple cider vinegar in a measuring jug. Add enough plant milk to reach the 300ml/½ pint mark. Stir well and leave at room temperature for about 5 minutes before using. Adjust the proportions to suit your recipe.

Nut butter

Nut butters such as smooth peanut butter, almond butter, cashew nut butter and seed butters such as tahini can be used in recipes where eggs are purely used to hold the mixture together, but don't produce such a firm set, so bakes such as cookies will have a softer or more crumbly texture. Rich in nutrients including protein, they provide a nutty flavour. Use 3 tablespoons of nut or seed butter to replace 1 egg.

Examples: Peanut Butter Cookies (page 112), Tahini Cookies (page 122).

Vegan mayonnaise

This is a great alternative to traditional mayonnaise. An emulsified product, it can be used to replace eggs in highly flavoured cakes. The plain versions contain tiny amounts of flavouring ingredients such as lemon juice and mustard, but these won't be noticeable in the bake. Make sure you only use the plain ones though, and avoid those with ingredients such as chilli or garlic. Only use in recipes specifically tested with vegan mayonnaise.

Example: Mocha Mayonnaise Cake (page 62).

Vegan egg replacer

Egg replacer is a commercial product, a fine powder made from a blend of potato starch, tapioca starch, raising agents and cellulose. It is usually sold in tubs; a small 135g/4¾oz tub contains the equivalent of 45 whole eggs. Reconstituted with water, it can be used instead of whole eggs, yolks and whites in cooking and baking and is best used in recipes specifically created for the product. As the powder is white, sponge cakes and custards will not be yellow (this can be advantageous if you want to create pastel-coloured sponges). When used instead of egg whites, the mixture will be softer and not suitable for piping.

BAKER'S TIPS

You'll find baker's tips on the individual bakes in this book to help and guide you, but there are a handful of simple rules that apply to all recipes.

- Get organised before you begin to bake. Make sure that you have all the ingredients you need for your chosen recipe. If you gather them together, weigh them out and place them on a tray or together in a corner on your worktop, hopefully you'll not put something in the oven then discover there was an ingredient that you forgot to add to the mixture.

- It is important to choose either metric or imperial measures when weighing out. Don't use a mixture, as the equivalents given are not exact.

- While you can sometimes convert a baking recipe by simply swapping ingredients such as butter with plant butter or vegan margarine, this won't always work. Dairy-free baking often requires a lot more tweaking, needing adjustments in quantities and different baking techniques, so it is preferable to use recipes specifically created for vegans.

- Many vegan cakes and bakes rely on vinegar or other acids such as lemon juice or vegan buttermilk and bicarbonate of soda or baking powder to make them rise and add lightness. As soon as they are mixed together, they start to activate. Always sift together the dry ingredients or stir them well before adding liquid ingredients, then mix quickly and put in the oven as soon as possible.

- For good results it is preferable to use the right-size cake tin for a recipe. Apart from Pandoro, which requires a special Pandoro tin, there are only a few different tins that you'll need for making cakes in this book: two 20–22cm (8–8½in) round shallow tins for layered sponges (you can use either size; 20cm/8in tins will produce slightly deeper sponges and will take a little longer to cook than something baked in 22cm/8½in tins), a 900g (2lb) loaf tin (it will hold about 1 litre/34fl oz of liquid and measure about 25 x 13cm/10 x 5½in; your tin may be a little shorter and fatter); 20cm (8in) and 23cm (9in) square tins, 20cm (8in) and 23cm (9in) round tins; a 22–23cm (8½–9in) loose-bottomed flan tin, a 28 x 18cm (11 x 7in) traybake tin, 12-hole non-stick cupcake tin, muffin tin and a Swiss roll tin. However, you don't have to use a round (or square) tin if that's what the recipe says. A 20cm (8in) round tin is roughly the same as an 18cm (7in) square one. Keep in mind that the volume of a square tin is roughly the same as a round tin that is 2cm (¾in) bigger.

- Get to know your oven; it's a good idea to test it with an oven thermometer to make sure it's at the correct heat and not hotter or cooler than the temperature setting. For most ovens, cakes and bakes should be cooked on the middle shelf.

CHAPTER ONE

Large Cakes

From quick-to-make homely Everyday Fruit Cake and Apple and Cranberry Loaf to light-as-air Victoria Sponge Cake or a gluten-free Cherry and Almond Cake, you'll find a cake to suit everyone and for every occasion in this chapter. Whether you are looking for something to serve at a simple afternoon tea with a few friends, or for a special event such as a birthday, Mother's Day or Christmas, this is your chance to create a delicious vegan-friendly bake. These are cakes that are sure to please.

Vegan cakes are usually made in a different way to traditional cakes containing eggs and dairy. You'll notice that there are only a few recipes here which begin by creaming fat and sugar together; instead, most are made by combining the dry ingredients together with wet ones such as plant milk and oil. Not only are the mixtures much faster and easier to make, the resulting cakes will rival any classic non-vegan recipe.

Whatever your favourite flavour – be it vanilla, coffee, chocolate or toffee, or fruit such as apple, banana or rhubarb – you'll find it here together with fabulous creamy-tasting fillings between the layers and toppings to add the finishing flourish. This chapter includes classics such as Sachertorte, Rich Fruit Cake and Classic Carrot Cake, as well as more modern creations such as Rose and Almond Cake and Lemon and Elderflower Sponge.

Victoria Sponge Cake

This beautifully simple baking classic was named after Queen Victoria, who apparently enjoyed a slice with afternoon tea. Traditionally made by creaming butter and sugar together, carefully beating in eggs, then folding in flour, this vegan version is so much easier to make and tastes every bit as good. This is the perfect centrepiece for a special tea table and with a generous filling of coconut cream and jam it is irresistible.

SERVES 8

400g/14oz self-raising white flour
2 tsp baking powder
225g/8oz caster sugar
400ml/14fl oz plant milk e.g., unsweetened soya or almond milk
160ml/5½fl oz rapeseed oil or sunflower oil
1 tbsp vanilla extract

For the cream and jam filling:
150ml/¼ pint whipped coconut cream (see Baker's Tips)
100g/3½oz good-quality strawberry jam
1 tsp icing sugar, for dusting

1 Preheat the oven to 180°C/fan oven 160°C/gas 4. Lightly grease two shallow 20cm (8in) or 22cm (8½in) round cake tins and line the bases with non-stick baking paper. Sift the flour and baking powder into a mixing bowl. Add the sugar and stir to mix, then make a hollow in the middle.

2 Mix the plant milk, oil and vanilla extract together in a jug with a fork. Add to the dry ingredients and quickly mix everything together. Divide the mixture equally between the two prepared tins.

3 Tap the tins on the work surface to stop the raising agent working too quickly, then bake for 18–20 minutes, or until

golden brown, well risen and springy when the top is gently pressed with a finger. Double-check by pushing a fine skewer into the middle of the sponges; it should come out clean.

4 Allow the cakes to cool in the tins for 5 minutes, then carefully turn out onto a wire rack and leave to cool completely. Peel off the baking paper.

5 Put one of the sponges onto a serving plate and spread evenly with whipped coconut cream. Beat the jam for a few seconds to soften it, then spoon and spread it over the top of the coconut cream. Top with the second sponge and dust the top with icing sugar. Keep chilled until ready to serve and store any leftovers in an airtight container in the fridge. Eat within 2 days of making.

BAKER'S TIPS

To make whipped coconut cream, chill a 400ml/14fl oz tin of full-fat coconut milk in the fridge for several hours or overnight. Carefully open the tin; the coconut cream will be at the top. Spoon out into a chilled bowl, leaving the watery coconut milk behind (you can use this in other recipes such as curries). Add 1 teaspoon of vanilla extract to the coconut cream, then whisk for a few minutes until soft peaks form. Use straight away.

Whipped coconut cream is a delicious cake filling but if you want to keep the cakes for longer or make them well ahead of time, make a vegan 'buttercream' instead: Beat 75g/2¾oz softened plant butter and 125g/4¼oz sifted icing sugar together until light and fluffy. Beat in 1 teaspoon of vanilla extract. Depending on the warmth of your kitchen, you may need to add a teaspoon or two of plant milk to make the buttercream a soft spreadable consistency. If you prefer a sweeter buttercream, beat in an extra 25g/1oz sifted icing sugar.

Classic Carrot Cake

A popular wedding cake in the 1970s, the originality of the carrot cake was that it was made with oil rather than butter, as well as its tangy not-too-sweet cream cheese frosting. In the last decade it has made a comeback and is often served as a trendy coffee-shop cake. Vegan cream cheese – a relatively new product – means that everyone can enjoy this cake.

SERVES 10

100g/3½oz walnut pieces
200ml/7fl oz rapeseed or sunflower oil
225g/8oz light muscovado or light brown soft sugar
finely grated zest of 1 orange, preferably unwaxed
200ml/7fl oz aquafaba (page 13)
300g/10½oz self-raising white flour
½ tsp baking powder
1¼ tsp bicarbonate of soda
2 tsp ground cinnamon
a pinch of salt
300g/10½oz finely grated carrots (3–4 medium carrots)
2 tsp lemon juice

For the filling and icing:
100g/3½oz plant butter (preferably unsalted) or vegan block
    margarine, softened
200g/7oz icing sugar
100g/3½oz full-fat vegan cream cheese alternative, at room
    temperature
finely grated zest of 1 orange, preferably unwaxed
1 tsp lemon juice

1   Put the walnut pieces on a baking tray and put in a cold oven. Heat the oven to 180°C/fan oven 160°C/gas 4 and bake the nuts for 5–7 minutes, or until they are lightly toasted and smell nutty; watch carefully as they burn easily. Remove from the oven. Lightly grease two shallow 20cm (8in) or 22cm (8½in) round cake tins and line the bases with non-stick baking paper.

2 Put the oil and sugar into a mixing bowl with the orange zest. Using an electric whisk, mix on low speed until blended, then continue whisking for 2 minutes. Gradually whisk in the aquafaba and whisk the mixture for a further minute.

3 Sift the flour, baking powder, bicarbonate of soda, cinnamon and salt into a bowl to mix, then re-sift over the sugar and oil mixture. Start folding in, then when half mixed, add the grated carrots, lemon juice and about two-thirds of the toasted walnuts (reserve the rest for decoration). Continue folding and mixing until everything is combined.

4 Quickly spoon and scrape the mixture equally between the two prepared tins. Bake for 35–40 minutes, or until the cakes are firm to the touch and a fine skewer inserted into the middle of the sponges comes out clean. Allow to cool in the tins for 10 minutes, then turn out and leave to cool on a wire rack. Peel off the baking paper.

5 While the cakes cool, make the mixture for the filling and icing. Put the plant butter or margarine in a mixing bowl and beat for a few seconds to soften, then sift over the icing sugar. Mix together then beat with a wooden spoon until creamy. Gently beat the vegan cream cheese to soften (so that it blends easily), then stir it into the butter and sugar mixture with the orange zest and lemon juice.

6 Spread slightly less than half of the icing over one of the cakes, then top with the other cake. Spread the rest of the icing over the top and decorate with the reserved walnuts. Store the cake in an airtight container and keep in the fridge until ready to serve. Eat within 4 days.

BAKER'S TIP

If you like a fruity carrot cake, put 75g/2¾oz sultanas in a small bowl and sprinkle with 2 tablespoons of orange juice. Leave them to soak for at least 1 hour, stirring occasionally to coat in the juice (or you can leave in the fridge overnight to make them really plump). Add to the mixture with the carrots in step 3.

Celebration Coconut Layer Cake

This triple-layer cake contains vegan coconut yogurt in the sponge and is filled and covered with a white frosting and a scattering of desiccated coconut which gives it a snowy look. It's the perfect Christmas cake alternative for those who don't like fruit cake.

SERVES 10

100ml/3½fl oz plant milk e.g., coconut 'drink' milk or soya milk
1 tsp cider vinegar
200g/7oz vegan coconut or soya yogurt
150ml/¼ pint rapeseed oil or sunflower oil
2 tsp vanilla extract
200g/7oz caster sugar
25g/1oz desiccated coconut
300g/10½oz plain white flour
1 tsp baking powder
1 tsp bicarbonate of soda
a pinch of salt

For the filling and frosting:
2 x 400g/14oz tins of full-fat coconut milk, chilled in the fridge overnight
1 tsp vanilla extract
1 tbsp icing sugar, sifted
200g/7oz desiccated coconut

1 Preheat the oven to 180°C/fan oven 160°C/gas 4. Lightly grease three shallow 18–20cm (7–8in) round cake tins and line the bases with non-stick baking paper.
2 For the sponges, mix the plant milk and cider vinegar together in a jug. Stir in the yogurt, followed by the oil and vanilla extract.
3 Put the sugar and desiccated coconut in a bowl. Sift over the flour, baking powder, bicarbonate of soda and salt. Stir

together, then make a hollow in the middle. Pour in the yogurt mixture and quickly mix everything together. Divide the mixture equally between the three prepared tins. Tap the tins on the work surface to stop the raising agents working too quickly.

4 Bake for 20 minutes, or until the tops are firm and a fine skewer inserted into the middle of the cakes comes out clean. Allow to cool in the tins for 5 minutes, then carefully turn out onto a wire rack and leave to cool completely. Peel off the baking paper.

5 For the filling and frosting, open the tins of chilled coconut milk and spoon the solidified cream into a chilled bowl (keep the watery coconut milk for another recipe). Add the vanilla extract and icing sugar and whisk together.

6 Place one of the sponges on a serving plate and spread a layer of the coconut frosting on top. Repeat with the two remaining sponges to make a three-layer cake. Spread the remaining frosting over the top and sides of the cake, cover the top and sides with the desiccated coconut, then chill until ready to serve. Once cut, store in an airtight container or cover with cling film (or plastic-free alternative) and keep in the fridge. Eat within 5 days.

BAKER'S TIP

The mixture can be cooked in two 20-22cm (8-8½in) round cake tins if you don't have three smaller ones. You will need to cook the sponges for a little longer; about 25 minutes in total.

VARIATION

For a chocolate coconut cake, use 250g/9oz plain white flour and 50g/1¾oz unsweetened cocoa powder instead of all plain white flour.

Light Fruit Cake

A beautifully simple cake, in which the fruit is soaked in hot water to make it really plump and moist. Although you could use block margarine in this recipe, I prefer plant butter here, which gives it a better flavour. The combination of wholemeal and plain white flour makes this a healthier bake without a heavy texture. Allow the cake to mature for a day or two before serving; you will find it gets moister and is easier to slice.

MAKES 8-10 SLICES

250g/9oz dried mixed fruit
150ml/¼ pint boiling water
45g/1½oz plant butter or vegan margarine
125g/4¼oz light brown soft sugar
1 tbsp cider vinegar
120ml/4fl oz plant milk e.g., unsweetened soya or oat milk
100g/3½oz plain white flour
100g/3½oz self-raising wholemeal flour
1 tsp ground cinnamon
1 tsp ground mixed spice
1 tsp bicarbonate of soda
a pinch of salt (optional)

1 Put the fruit in a saucepan and pour over the boiling water. Add the butter or margarine (just leave it to melt in the heat), cover the pan with a lid and leave for 2 hours.
2 When the fruit has soaked, preheat the oven to 180°C/fan oven 160°C/gas 4. Lightly grease a deep 20cm (8in) square cake tin and line the base with non-stick baking paper.
3 Gently heat the soaked fruit in the saucepan over a low heat until the butter or margarine has re-melted (the mixture should be barely warm; don't let it boil). Remove the pan from the heat and stir in the sugar and cider vinegar followed by the plant milk.

4 Mix the flours, spices, bicarbonate of soda and salt (if using) together in a bowl. Sift the dry mixture over the fruit mixture, adding the bran left in the sieve. Quickly mix everything together.

5 Spoon and scrape the mixture into the prepared tin, spreading it to the corners. Bake for 40 minutes, or until the top is firm and lightly browned and a fine skewer inserted into the middle of the cake comes out clean.

6 Leave the cake to cool in the tin for 15 minutes, then turn out onto a wire rack and leave to cool completely. Wrap in greaseproof or baking paper, then in foil, and leave for a day or two before thickly slicing and serving.

BAKER'S TIPS

Add a subtle orange flavour to the cake by paring a large piece of rind or two from an orange (preferably unwaxed). Place in the bottom of the pan before adding the fruit and boiling water. Discard before making the cake.

Mixed spice is a combination of several spices. You can buy it ready-made or prepare your own by mixing 1 tablespoon of ground allspice, 1 tablespoon of ground cinnamon, 1 tablespoon of ground nutmeg, 2 teaspoons of ground mace, 1 teaspoon of ground ginger and 1 teaspoon of ground coriander. Store in an airtight jar; it will keep for up to a year. If you prefer, instead of mixed spice, you can add an extra teaspoon of ground cinnamon or 1 teaspoon of ground ginger to the cake mixture.

Look for dried fruit mixes which contain fruits such as cranberries and apricots; these are great in a vegan diet as they provide B-vitamins and iron.

Everyday Fruit Cake

This 'plain' fruit cake is made by the rubbing-in method and has a lovely crunchy sugar topping. The recipe has been around for at least a century, although it was traditionally made with dairy not plant-based milk and butter. It originated in East Anglia where it is known as 'vinegar cake', made in times when hens were 'off lay' (see Note). Despite the name, any trace of vinegar completely disappears during baking.

MAKES 10 SLICES

175g/6oz self-raising white flour
175g/6oz plain wholemeal flour
1 tsp ground mixed spice (see Baker's Tip on page 27)
a pinch of salt
125g/4¼oz cold plant butter or vegan block margarine, cubed
100g/3½oz light muscovado or light brown soft sugar
375g/13oz mixed dried fruit
2 tbsp golden syrup
200ml/7fl oz plant milk e.g., unsweetened soya or oat milk
1 tsp bicarbonate of soda
2 tbsp cider vinegar
1 tbsp demerara sugar

1 Preheat the oven to 170°C/fan oven 150°C/gas 3. Lightly grease a 23cm (9in) square cake tin and line the base with non-stick baking paper.
2 Sift the flours, mixed spice and salt into a mixing bowl, adding the bran left in the sieve. Rub in the butter or margarine with your fingertips until the mixture resembles fine breadcrumbs, then stir in the sugar and dried fruit. Make a hollow in the middle.
3 Put the golden syrup in a small bowl and mix with a few tablespoons of the milk. Mix the bicarbonate of soda with 1 tablespoon of the milk in another small bowl.

4 Stir the vinegar into the rest of the milk in a large jug (it will curdle), then add the bicarbonate of soda mixture; it will froth up to about 3 times its original volume, so make sure the jug is big enough. Pour the frothing milk into the dry ingredients, add the golden syrup and milk blend, then quickly mix everything until just combined; the mixture will be soft and lumpy.

5 Pour and scrape the mixture into the prepared tin and level the top. Sprinkle the top with the demerara sugar and bake for about 40 minutes, or until the top is golden brown and a fine skewer inserted into the middle of the cake comes out clean.

6 Put the cake on a wire rack and leave to cool in the tin for 30 minutes, then turn out onto a wire rack and leave to cool completely. Wrap in greaseproof or baking paper, then wrap in foil and leave to mature for at least a day before slicing.

BAKER'S TIPS

Cooked in a 23cm (9in) square cake tin, this cake is fairly shallow; about 4cm (1½in) high, ideal for cutting into slices. If you want a deeper cake, cook it in a 20cm (8in) square tin, allowing an extra 10 minutes cooking time and covering the top after 40 minutes to prevent it over-browning.

Note: With eggs available in supermarkets all year round, it's easy to forget that chickens, like all birds, naturally avoid laying eggs in the winter months when chicks would have the lowest chance of survival. Decades ago, smallholders would allow their chickens to rest and recuperate during this time. Because the laying cycle of chickens depends on the number of daylight hours, commercial producers use artificial light to stimulate egg laying.

Raisin and Cinnamon Malt Teabread

This quick and simple cake is made using bran cereal which contains barley malt extract. High in fibre, it has a lovely moist texture and slices beautifully – few will guess that it's based on a breakfast cereal.

MAKES 8-10 SLICES

100g/3½oz bran cereal, such as All-bran
250g/9oz raisins or mixed dried fruit
300ml/½ pint plant milk e.g., unsweetened soya or oat milk
50g/1¾oz light muscovado or light brown soft sugar
100g/3½oz self-raising white flour
2 tsp ground cinnamon
½ tsp baking powder
plant butter or vegan margarine, to serve (optional)

1 Put the bran cereal in a bowl and add the fruit. Pour over the milk, cover the bowl with cling film (or plastic-free alternative) or a pan lid and leave to soak at room temperature for 1 hour, or overnight in the fridge, if you prefer.

2 Preheat the oven to 180°C/fan oven 160°C/gas 4. Lightly grease a 23cm (9in) square cake tin and line the base and sides with non-stick baking paper. Stir the sugar into the soaked bran and fruit mixture.

3 Sift over the flour, cinnamon and baking powder. Gently fold in but do not overmix. Spoon and scrape the mixture into the prepared cake tin.

4 Bake the cake for 45–50 minutes until risen and firm. If the top starts to get too brown, cover it with a piece of foil about 30 minutes into the cooking time.

5 Put the cake on a wire rack and leave to cool in the tin for 15 minutes, then turn out onto the wire rack and leave to cool

completely. Serve thickly sliced, spread with a little plant butter or vegan margarine, if you like.

VARIATION

For a tropical fruit teabread, use 250g/9oz dried tropical fruit, such as dried pineapple, papaya and mango, chopped into smaller pieces if necessary. Instead of oat milk, use coconut 'drink' milk (page 11) or almond milk.

Rich Fruit Cake

Packed with boozy fruit and spices, this fruit cake is perfect for Christmas or for those who simply love a rich cake. It can be made up to eight weeks in advance and should be left to mature for at least two weeks before eating. Leave it plain or decorate with traditional almond paste (marzipan) and Royal icing. Choose good-quality mixed fruit – blends which also contain mixed peel and dried cranberries are perfect – and remember to soak the fruit for at least 8 hours in advance.

MAKES 16 SLICES

450g/1lb mixed dried fruit

75g/2¾oz glacé cherries, preferably morello glacé cherries, quartered

100ml/3½fl oz rum or brandy, plus extra for 'feeding'

100ml/3½fl oz plant milk e.g., unsweetened soya or oat milk

2 tbsp cider vinegar

175g/6oz plant butter or vegan block margarine, softened

175g/6oz light or dark muscovado or brown soft sugar

1 tbsp black treacle or molasses

finely grated zest of 1 orange, preferably unwaxed

finely grated zest of 1 lemon, preferably unwaxed

50g/1¾oz ground almonds

350g/12oz plain white flour

¾ tsp bicarbonate of soda

1 tsp ground mixed spice

1 tsp ground cinnamon

75g/2¾oz blanched almonds, chopped

For the almond paste:
200g/7oz icing sugar, plus extra for kneading and rolling out
275g/9¾oz ground almonds
1½ tbsp rum, brandy or cooled boiled water
¼ tsp almond extract (optional)
½ tsp lemon juice
4 tbsp apricot jam, warmed and sieved

For the Royal icing:
130ml/4½fl oz aquafaba (page 13)
500g/1lb 2oz icing sugar, sifted
2 tsp vegetable glycerine (optional)

1   Put the dried fruit and glacé cherries in a bowl. Pour over the rum or brandy and stir, then cover and leave at room temperature for at least 8 hours and up to 24 hours. If possible, give the mixture an occasional stir.

2   Preheat the oven to 150°C/fan oven 130°C/gas 2. Lightly grease a 20cm (8in) round deep cake tin and line the base and sides with a double layer of non-stick baking paper. Pour the milk into a jug and stir in the vinegar – it will thicken and curdle slightly. Leave to stand at room temperature.

3   Put the plant butter or margarine, sugar, treacle (or molasses) and orange and lemon zest into a bowl and beat together until light and creamy. Stir in the ground almonds.

4   Sift the flour, bicarbonate of soda, mixed spice and cinnamon into a bowl to mix, then sift again, this time over the butter and sugar mixture. Add the milk, soaked fruit and any leftover liquid and the chopped almonds and fold in until everything is just mixed.

5   Spoon and scrape the mixture into the prepared tin and level the top with the back of the spoon. Tap the tin on the work surface to stop the raising agent working too quickly, then bake

for 2–2¼ hours, or until a fine skewer inserted into the middle of the cake comes out clean. If necessary, cover the top with foil towards the end of cooking to prevent it getting too brown.

6   Remove the cake from the oven and place on a wire rack. Leave the cake to cool in the tin, then turn out, but do not remove the baking paper as it helps to keep the cake moist. When the cake is completely cold, prick the top all over with a fine skewer and spoon over 2 tablespoons of rum or brandy. Leave for an hour or two then wrap in non-stick baking paper (or greaseproof paper) and foil.

7   Store the cake, the right way up, in a cool dry place for a week. Unwrap and spoon over a further 2 tablespoons of rum or brandy, then re-wrap and store the cake upside down, so that the alcohol moistens and softens the top of the cake and helps keep it flat. Leave for a further week; the cake will now be ready to eat, or can be kept for up to 2 months.

8   To make the almond paste, sift the icing sugar into a bowl. Add the ground almonds and stir to mix. Add the rum, brandy or water, almond extract (if using) and lemon juice. Stir together to mix to a thick stiff paste, adding a little more icing sugar or a few more drops of alcohol to get the right consistency. Lightly knead on a surface dusted with icing sugar until smooth.

9   Place the unwrapped cake on a cake board or flat plate and brush with the apricot glaze in a thin, even layer. Dust the work surface with a little more icing sugar and roll out the almond paste into a circle about 40cm (16in) across. Using the rolling pin, carefully lift it on top of the cake. Smooth the almond paste over the cake using the palms of your hands, rubbing any small cracks together, then trim with a sharp knife. Leave for at least 24 hours or up to 3 days before icing.

10 To make the Royal icing, whisk the aquafaba with an electric whisk until foamy, then gradually add 400g/14oz of the icing

sugar. Whisk on high speed until thick and glossy. Whisk in the glycerine, then gradually add the rest of the icing sugar until soft peaks are formed; you may not need it all. Spread the icing over the top and sides of the cake, decorate as liked and leave to set.

BAKER'S TIPS

You can soak the fruit in orange juice instead of alcohol if you prefer. Don't use this to soak the cake after baking though; just leave this step out.

The cake can be covered with fondant icing rather than Royal icing; most brands are vegan, but always check the ingredients list as some may contain gelatine.

Orchard Fruit Cake

This fruity bake is a cross between a cake and a flapjack and is a great way to use fresh fruit when in season or if you have a glut of home-grown. It contains no added sugar and relies on the sweetness and flavour of the fruit, so is perfect if you are looking for a healthier bake.

MAKES 12 SLICES

100g/3½oz skinned hazelnuts or walnuts, roughly chopped
450g/1lb ripe eating apples or pears (or a mixture of both)
150g/5½oz rolled (porridge) oats
100g/3½oz desiccated coconut
150g/5½oz dried dates, chopped into 1cm (½in) pieces
140g/5oz self-raising white flour
a pinch of salt (optional)
200ml/7fl oz rapeseed oil or sunflower oil

1 Put the nuts on a baking tray and put in a cold oven. Heat to 180°C/fan oven 160°C/gas 4 and bake the nuts for 5–7 minutes, or until they smell nutty; watch carefully as they burn easily. Remove from the oven and leave to cool.

2 Lightly grease a deep 23cm (9in) square cake tin and line the base with non-stick baking paper. Quarter, core and peel the apples and/or pears, then coarsely grate.

3 Put the toasted nuts, oats, coconut, chopped dates, flour and salt (if using) in a mixing bowl and stir together. Add the grated fruit and oil and mix everything together.

4 Spoon and scrape the mixture into the prepared tin and level the top, gently pressing with the back of the spoon. Bake for 40 minutes until firm to the touch and lightly browned.

5 Put the cake on a wire rack and leave to cool in the tin, then turn out and cut into squares. Store in an airtight tin and eat within 4 days.

Cherry and Almond Cake

Most of us know someone who is gluten-intolerant and this is perfect for those occasions when you need to bake a cake for family or friends with different nutritional needs. If you are baking for a coeliac, make sure that you avoid cross-contamination with products which contain gluten.

SERVES 10

200g/7oz glacé cherries, preferably morello glacé cherries
300ml/½ pint plant milk e.g., unsweetened almond milk, at
   room temperature
1 tbsp cider vinegar
½ tsp almond extract (optional)
200g/7oz gluten-free self-raising white flour
1 tsp gluten-free baking powder
150g/5½oz ground almonds
100g/3½oz caster sugar
100ml/3½fl oz melted coconut oil
1 tsp icing sugar, for dusting

1 Rinse the glacé cherries in a sieve under cold running water to remove some of the syrup. Pat dry with kitchen paper, then cut into quarters and leave on a plate to air-dry a little. Pour the plant milk into a jug. Add the vinegar and almond extract (if using) and stir well. Leave to stand for at least 5 minutes; the mixture will curdle.

2 Preheat the oven to 180°C/fan oven 160°C/gas 4. Lightly grease a 23cm (9in) round cake tin and line the base with non-stick baking paper.

3 Sift the flour and baking powder into a bowl. Add the cherries and stir to coat in the flour. Add the ground almonds and sugar and stir again to mix all the dry ingredients. Make a hollow in the middle.

4 Add the melted coconut to the plant milk and stir briefly with a fork. Add to the dry ingredients and mix until just combined. Spoon and scrape the mixture into the prepared tin and level the top with the back of a spoon. Bake for 45 minutes, or until a fine skewer inserted into the middle of the cake comes out fairly clean.

5 Put the cake on a wire rack and leave to cool in the tin for 15 minutes, then turn out onto the wire rack to cool. Peel off the baking paper. Dust the top with icing sugar before slicing and serving.

BAKER'S TIP

Many supermarkets sell morello glacé cherries; they have a tangy sweet flavour and are a darker red colour than ordinary glacé cherries. Rinsing and drying the cherries, then coating them in the flour mixture, will ensure that they don't sink to the bottom of the cake during baking.

Apple and Cranberry Loaf

I love this cake for its simplicity as it only takes a few minutes to mix all the ingredients together. When it comes to egg alternatives, apple puree is the vegan baker's ally and it's worth making your own and freezing in batches (page 12). Because apple puree gives a soft moist texture to the finished bake, it can be used to replace some or all of the fat you would otherwise need to add in baking.

MAKES 8-10 SLICES

175g/6oz unsweetened apple puree (page 12)
75g/2¾oz dried cranberries
75ml/2½fl oz sunflower or rapeseed oil
125g/4¼oz caster sugar
1 tsp vanilla extract
1 tbsp cider vinegar
200g/7oz self-raising white flour
1 tsp ground ginger
½ tsp baking powder
½ tsp bicarbonate of soda
a pinch of salt (optional)

To finish:
1 tsp icing sugar
¼ tsp ground cinnamon

1 Preheat the oven to 190°C/fan oven 170°C/gas 5. Lightly grease a 900g (2lb) loaf tin and line the base with non-stick baking paper.

2 Put the apple puree, cranberries, oil, sugar and vanilla extract in a mixing bowl and stir together until combined. Stir in the vinegar.

3 Sift the flour, ginger, baking powder, bicarbonate of soda and salt (if using) together into a bowl. Sift again over the wet

ingredients. Stir everything together quickly (don't overmix) and bake straight away as the bicarbonate of soda will start reacting with the vinegar, raising the mixture.

4   Spoon and scrape the mixture into the tin. Put into the oven and immediately lower the temperature to 180°C/fan oven 160°C/gas 4. Bake for about 50 minutes, or until well risen, light brown and firm, and a fine skewer inserted into the middle of the loaf comes out clean.

5   Put the loaf on a wire rack and leave to cool in the tin for 15 minutes, then carefully turn out onto the wire rack and leave to cool completely. Mix the icing sugar and ground cinnamon and sift over the top of the loaf. Serve thickly sliced.

BAKER'S TIP

Sifting the flour mixture twice helps to blend the spice and raising agents into the flour as well as removing any lumps and adding air to lighten the cake.

Toffee Apple Cake

This is a great cake to serve on Bonfire night or warm as a dessert in autumn as the days shorten and nights start to get a little chillier. Serve it with vegan crème fraîche, which works well with the sticky texture and sweet toffee flavour, or hot vegan custard.

SERVES 8-10

4 medium well-flavoured eating apples, such as Cox or Russet
250g/9oz light muscovado or brown soft sugar
175g/6oz unsweetened apple puree (page 12)
75g/2¾oz plant butter or vegan block margarine, melted
1 tbsp cider vinegar
200g/7oz self-raising white flour
½ tsp baking powder
½ tsp bicarbonate of soda
a pinch of salt
vegan crème fraîche alternative (e.g., oat fraîche) or hot
    vegan custard, to serve (optional)

1 Preheat the oven to 190°C/fan oven 170°C/gas 5. Lightly grease a deep 20cm (8in) round cake tin and line the base with non-stick baking paper.
2 Quarter, core and peel the apples. Slice each quarter into 4 or 5 thin slices. Put 100g/3½oz of the sugar in a bowl, add the apple slices and toss until coated. Starting from the outside and working inwards, arrange the apple slices over the base of the prepared tin.
3 Put the apple puree, melted butter or margarine and remaining 150g/5½oz sugar in a mixing bowl and whisk together until combined. Stir in the vinegar.
4 Sift the flour, baking powder, bicarbonate of soda and salt together into a bowl. Sift again over the wet ingredients and quickly mix together.

5 Spoon and scrape the mixture into the tin, taking care not to disturb the sliced apples. Put into the oven and immediately lower the temperature to 180°C/fan oven 160°C/gas 4. Bake for about 45 minutes, or until a fine skewer inserted into the middle of the cake comes out clean.

6 Put the cake on a wire rack and leave to cool in the tin for 15 minutes, then carefully turn out onto the wire rack. Remove the baking paper and cut into wedges to serve. If intended as a dessert, serve slightly warm with hot vegan custard or vegan crème fraîche.

VARIATION

For a sticky pear and chocolate cake, use dessert pears instead of apples and substitute 3 tablespoons unsweetened cocoa powder for 3 tablespoons of the flour.

Rose and Almond Cake

Almond milk's subtle nutty character works well in this delicately-flavoured cake. Traditionally-made 'proper' Turkish delight doesn't contain gelatine, but do double-check that the one you buy is vegan.

SERVES 8-10

350g/12oz self-raising white flour
2 tsp baking powder
a pinch of salt (optional)
50g/1¾oz ground almonds
200g/7oz caster sugar
400ml/14fl oz almond milk
150ml/¼ pint rapeseed oil or sunflower oil
1 tbsp vanilla extract
2 tsp–2 tbsp rose water, to taste (see Baker's Tips)

For the rose frosting:
50g/1¾oz dairy-free margarine, softened
50g/1¾oz white vegetable fat, at room temperature
300g/10½oz icing sugar, sifted
1–3 tsp rose water
2 drops of pink food colouring
rose-flavoured Turkish delight (not chocolate-coated!) or
   dried edible rose petals

1 Preheat the oven to 180°C/fan oven 160°C/gas 4. Grease two 20cm (8in) or 22cm (8½in) round cake tins and line the bases with non-stick baking paper.
2 Sift the flour, baking powder and salt (if using) into a mixing bowl. Stir in the ground almonds and sugar. Make a hollow in the middle.

3 Put the milk, oil, vanilla extract and rose water in a jug. Stir the mixture, then add to the dry ingredients and quickly mix everything together; don't overmix – it should be just blended.

4 Divide the mixture equally between the two tins and level the tops. Tap the tins on the work surface to stop the raising agents working too quickly. Bake for 18–20 minutes, or until the tops are springy and a fine skewer inserted into the middle of the cakes comes out clean.

5 Place the tins on a wire rack and leave to cool in the tins for 10 minutes, then turn out onto the wire rack and leave to cool completely. Carefully peel off the baking paper.

6 Meanwhile, make the rose frosting: beat the margarine and white vegetable fat together until creamy. Add half the icing sugar and gradually beat in, then add the remaining icing sugar, rose water and food colouring and beat until light and creamy.

7 Spread the top of one of the cakes with half of the rose frosting, then top with the second cake. Spread the remaining frosting over the top of the cake and decorate with chopped Turkish delight or edible rose petals.

BAKER'S TIPS

Rose water varies in strength, so check yours and adjust the amount you use accordingly; the bottle should give you some indication of how much to use.

To make Turkish delight, lightly grease a shallow 18cm (7in) square tin and line the base with non-stick baking paper. Put 400g/14oz granulated sugar in a saucepan with ½ teaspoon of cream of tartar. Stir in 400ml/14fl oz cold water. Heat gently, stirring until the sugar dissolves, then turn up the heat and boil for 10–15 minutes, or until the mixture reaches 118°C on a sugar thermometer. Blend 100g/3½oz cornflour with 100ml/3½fl oz cold water. Slowly add to the sugar syrup, stirring all the time. Continue to simmer, stirring frequently until the mixture is thick enough to see a clear line though it with a spoon; this can take up to 40 minutes. Test the mixture by dropping a small amount into chilled water; it should form a ball that feels springy when squeezed. Turn off the heat and stir in ½–2 teaspoons rose water and a drop of pink food colouring or 2 tablespoons of rose syrup. Pour into the tin and leave until cold. Mix 3 tablespoons of icing sugar with 1 teaspoon of cornflour and sift onto a board. Turn out the Turkish delight and cut into squares, coating each with the icing sugar mixture. Leave for a few hours to dry and harden, then store in an airtight container for up to a week.

Rhubarb Crumble and Custard Cake

Rhubarb is one of the few fresh fruits (well technically it's a vegetable) that is only available during the spring months but it is sold in tins throughout the year; perfect for this delicious sponge which is finished with a biscuity crumble topping.

SERVES 8-10

For the crumble:
60g/2¼oz plain white flour
½ tsp ground ginger
40g/1½oz cold plant butter or vegan block margarine
25g/1oz demerara sugar

For the sponge:
375g/13oz self-raising white flour
25g/1oz custard powder
2 tsp baking powder
225g/8oz caster sugar
350ml/12fl oz plant milk e.g., unsweetened soya or oat milk
150ml/¼ pint rapeseed oil or sunflower oil
1 tbsp vanilla extract
2 tbsp rhubarb syrup (from the tin)
100g/3½oz tinned rhubarb, thoroughly drained

For the frosting:
175g/6oz plant butter or margarine, softened
400g/14oz icing sugar, sifted
1-2 tbsp rhubarb syrup (from the tin)
1-2 drops of pink paste food colouring

1 Preheat the oven to 180°C/fan oven 160°C/gas 4. Lightly grease two shallow 20cm (8in) or 22cm (8½in) round cake tins and line the bases with non-stick baking paper. Place a piece of non-stick baking paper in the bottom of a baking tray.
2 For the crumble, sift the flour and ground ginger into a bowl. Cut the plant butter or margarine into small cubes and rub into

the flour until the mixture resembles breadcrumbs. Stir in the demerara sugar. Spread out the crumble mixture in an even layer on the lined baking tray. Bake for 8–10 minutes, or until lightly browned. Remove from the oven and leave to cool.

3   Meanwhile, make the sponge: Sift the flour, custard powder and baking powder into a mixing bowl. Stir in the caster sugar and make a hollow in the middle. Put the milk, oil, vanilla extract and rhubarb syrup in a jug. Stir briefly, then add to the dry ingredients with the rhubarb. Quickly mix together, stirring until just combined. Divide the mixture equally between the prepared tins, levelling the tops.

4   Bake for 18–20 minutes, or until the tops are golden brown and springy and a fine skewer inserted into the middle of each sponge comes out clean. Put the cake tins on a wire rack and leave to cool in the tins for 10 minutes, then turn out onto the wire rack and leave to cool. Carefully peel the baking paper from the bases of the cakes.

5   While the cakes are cooling, make the frosting. Put the plant butter or margarine in a mixing bowl and beat for a minute to soften. Add half the icing sugar and 1 tablespoon of the rhubarb syrup and mix together, then stir in the rest of the icing sugar. Beat for a minute or two until light and fluffy. Add the remaining tablespoon of rhubarb if needed, to make a spreadable frosting.

6   Divide the frosting in half. Beat the food colouring into one half to colour it pink. Take the bottom layer of the cake and spread with the pink frosting, then place the second cake on top. Spread the uncoloured frosting over the top of the cake and sprinkle with the crumble. Serve cut into wedges.

BAKER'S TIP

If you want to leave out the crumble topping and just make a rhubarb cake, make half quantity of the frosting and use it as a cake filling only. Dust the top with icing sugar to serve.

BAKING IT VEGAN

Lemon and Elderflower Sponge

This generous cake is ideal for a special occasion, such as a birthday or baby shower. It would also make a pretty Easter cake decorated with tiny speckled sugar-coated chocolate eggs. If liked, each cake can be cut into two horizontally, then sandwiched back together with the lemon and elderflower curd to make an impressive cake with four layers.

SERVES 10-12

For the elderflower syrup:
40g/1½oz caster sugar
6 tbsp elderflower cordial

For the sponge:
400g/14oz self-raising white flour
2 tsp baking powder
250g/9oz caster sugar
finely grated zest of 2 lemons, preferably unwaxed
300ml/½ pint plant milk e.g., unsweetened almond or soya milk
120ml/4fl oz rapeseed oil or sunflower oil
2 tbsp elderflower syrup (see above)

For the lemon and elderflower curd:
30g/1oz cornflour
4 tbsp water
6 tbsp lemon juice
125g/4¼oz caster sugar
3 tbsp elderflower cordial
5 tbsp soya cream
10g/⅓oz plant butter or vegan block margarine
a pinch of salt

For the frosting:
100g/3½oz plant butter or vegan block margarine, softened
225g/8oz icing sugar, sifted
2 tbsp lemon and elderflower curd (see above)

1   Preheat the oven to 180°C/fan oven 160°C/gas 4. Lightly grease two shallow 20cm (8in) or 22cm (8½in) round cake tins and line the bases with non-stick baking paper. To make the elderflower syrup, put the sugar and elderflower cordial in a small saucepan. Bring to the boil, stirring occasionally to dissolve the sugar, then simmer for 2–3 minutes until slightly thickened. Turn off the heat.

2   For the sponges, sift the flour and baking powder into a bowl, then stir in the sugar and lemon zest. Put the plant milk, oil and syrup (it's fine if it's still hot) in a jug, stir, then add to the dry ingredients and quickly mix together. Divide evenly between the prepared tins.

3   Bake for 30–35 minutes. The sponges should be springy to the touch and a fine skewer inserted into the middle of each sponge should come out clean. Put the cake tins on a wire rack and leave to cool in the tins for 5 minutes, then turn out onto the wire rack. Slowly drizzle the remaining elderflower syrup over the sponges while they are still warm. Leave to cool, then remove the baking paper.

4   To make the lemon and elderflower curd, put the cornflour in a small heavy-based saucepan and blend with a little of the water. Gradually stir in the rest of the water, then add the lemon juice, sugar and cordial. Slowly bring to the boil and simmer for 1 minute until thickened. Remove from the heat and stir in the cream, butter and salt. Spoon into a clean jar and put on the lid. Leave to cool, then chill in the fridge until ready to use.

5   For the frosting, beat the butter or margarine in a bowl until creamy, then gradually mix in the icing sugar. Beat until light and fluffy, then beat in the curd. The frosting needs to be an easy-to-spread consistency, so if it is a bit soft at this stage (this will depend on the warmth of your kitchen and the thickness of your lemon curd), beat in a little more sifted icing sugar.

6 To assemble, put one of the cakes on a serving plate and top with 6–8 tablespoons of the lemon and elderflower curd, spreading it evenly to the edges of the cake. Place the second cake on top. Cover the top and sides with the frosting, then decorate as liked.

BAKER'S TIP

You won't need all the lemon and elderflower curd for the cake filling. Store the rest in the fridge; it will keep for up to 2 weeks and is delicious on hot toast!

Lime and Coconut Sponge

Desiccated coconut gives this zesty lime sponge a great texture and is used instead of some of the flour. The sponge layers are filled with a lime curd made from coconut milk, which gives it a smooth silky texture and distinctive coconut flavour. If liked, the lime curd can be made the day before.

SERVES 8-10

300g/10½oz caster sugar
finely grated zest of 2 limes, preferably unwaxed, and the
   juice of 1
475g/1lb self-raising white flour
1½ tsp baking powder
25g/1oz desiccated coconut
150ml/¼ pint rapeseed or sunflower oil
250ml/8½fl oz cold water

For the coconut and lime curd filling:
5 limes
3 tbsp cornflour
400ml/14fl oz tin of full-fat coconut milk
100g/3½oz caster sugar

For the lime topping (optional):
150g/5½oz icing sugar
juice of ½–1 lime
2 tbsp desiccated coconut or toasted coconut flakes,
   for sprinkling

1   Preheat the oven to 190°C/fan oven 170°C/gas 5. Lightly grease two 20cm (8in) or 22cm (8½in) round sandwich tins and line the bases with non-stick baking paper.

2   Put the caster sugar and grated lime zest in a large mixing bowl. Sift over the flour and baking powder, add the desiccated coconut and stir until everything is combined. Make a hollow in the

middle. Put the oil, water and lime juice in a jug and stir. Pour into the hollow in the dry ingredients and mix everything together.

3   Working quickly, divide the mixture evenly between the prepared tins and bake for 18–20 minutes, or until well risen and light golden brown; when the top is gently pressed with a finger it should feel springy.

4   Put the cakes on a wire rack and leave to cool in the tins for 5 minutes, then turn out onto the wire rack and leave to cool completely. Remove the baking paper.

5   Make the coconut and lime curd. Finely grate the zest of 2 of the limes. Pare the rind of 1 lime and squeeze out the juice from all 5 limes. Put the cornflour into a small heavy-based saucepan and blend to a paste with a little of the juice. Stir in the remaining juice and the coconut milk, then add the caster sugar and the zested and pared lime rind. Bring to the boil and simmer uncovered for about 45 minutes, stirring frequently, until the mixture is well-reduced and thick. Remove the pared strips of lime rind. Spoon about 7 tablespoons (the amount you will need for the filling) into a bowl and the rest into a clean jar.

6   Spread the reserved lime curd over one of the sponges and place the other sponge on top. If you are icing the cake, make the lime topping. Sift the icing sugar into a bowl and stir in enough lime juice to make a thick pourable icing. Spoon and spread over the top of the cake; let it dribble over the sides if you like, then sprinkle with desiccated coconut or toasted coconut flakes. Allow to set before serving.

BAKER'S TIP

Store the jar of lime curd you don't need for the filling in the fridge; use within 2 weeks.

Lemon Drizzle Cake

A well-known afternoon-tea favourite, this light lemon sponge has a crunchy sweet and sharp citrus and sugar topping. Here it's made in a traditional loaf shape, but you can make it in a round tin if you prefer.

MAKES 8 SLICES

5 tbsp rapeseed or sunflower oil, plus extra for greasing
200g/7oz caster sugar
finely grated zest of 2 lemons, preferably unwaxed
250g/9oz plain white flour
1 tsp bicarbonate of soda
a pinch of salt (optional)
1 tbsp lemon juice
220ml/7½fl oz plant milk e.g., unsweetened almond or
    soya milk

For the sugar topping:
4 tbsp granulated sugar
juice of 2 lemons (about 4 tbsp)

1   Preheat the oven to 190°C/fan oven 170°C/gas 5. Lightly grease a 900g (2lb) loaf tin and line the base with non-stick baking paper.
2   Put the oil, caster sugar and lemon zest in a mixing bowl and stir together. Sift over the flour, bicarbonate of soda and salt (if using).
3   Stir the lemon juice into the plant milk and add to the bowl. Quickly mix everything together, then pour and scrape the mixture into the prepared tin.
4   Bake for 35–45 minutes, or until well risen and golden brown. Check the cake is cooked by inserting a fine skewer into the middle; it should come out clean. Put the cake on a wire rack and leave to cool in the tin for 10 minutes.

5 Meanwhile, for the sugar topping, mix the sugar and lemon juice together in a bowl; some but not all of the sugar will dissolve. Carefully turn out the cake, peel off the baking paper, then place the cake the right way up on a wire rack set over a plate or small tray. Make about 20 holes over the top of the cake with a very fine skewer or cocktail stick.

6 Slowly and gradually, spoon the lemon sugar mixture over the cake, stopping now and then to allow it to penetrate the sponge. Leave the cake to cool and the topping to crystallise. Cut into generous slices to serve.

BAKER'S TIP

For a lemon and lime drizzle cake, replace one of the lemons with a lime; use the finely grated zest in the sponge and the juice for the sugar topping.

Citrus Polenta Cake

This cake has an almost 'sandy' texture and is delicious served with vegan crème fraîche, such as 'oat fraîche' or vegan coconut yogurt. It is gluten-free, so is ideal for sharing with friends who have different nutritional needs.

SERVES 8-10

2 tbsp plus 1 tsp chia seeds
275ml/9½fl oz unsweetened almond milk
finely grated zest and juice of 1 lemon, preferably unwaxed
finely grated zest and juice of 1 large orange, preferably unwaxed
250g/9oz fine polenta or fine cornmeal
250g/9oz ground almonds
2 tbsp ground arrowroot
2 tsp baking powder
½ tsp bicarbonate of soda
a pinch of salt (optional)
175ml/6fl oz maple syrup or maple and carob syrup blend
3 tbsp coconut oil, melted, plus extra for greasing

For the syrup topping:
finely grated zest and juice of 1 large orange, preferably unwaxed
1 tbsp lemon juice
50g/1¾oz coconut sugar or light brown soft sugar

1   Put the chia seeds in a large jug and pour over half of the almond milk. Leave to soak for at least 20 minutes; the seeds will swell and form a sticky gel. Add 2 teaspoons of the lemon juice to the rest of the milk and stir to mix. Leave at room temperature.

2   Preheat the oven to 190°C/fan oven 170°C/gas 5. Lightly grease a 20cm (8in) round cake tin with coconut oil and line the base with non-stick baking paper.

3 Put the cornmeal and ground almonds into a large mixing bowl and sift over the arrowroot, baking powder, bicarbonate of soda and salt (if using). Stir together until well mixed, then make a hollow in the middle.

4 Whisk the chia seed mixture with a fork, then add the rest of the milk and the orange and lemon zest and juices, followed by the maple syrup and melted coconut oil. Stir and add to the dry ingredients. Mix everything together, then spoon and scrape the mixture into the prepared tin.

5 Bake for 45–50 minutes, or until the top is golden brown and a fine skewer inserted into the middle of the cake comes out clean. Remove from the oven and leave to cool in the tin for 15 minutes.

6 Meanwhile, make the syrup topping: mix the orange zest and juice, lemon juice and sugar together in a jug, stirring until the sugar is dissolved. Drizzle evenly over the warm cake. Leave for a further 5 minutes, then carefully remove the cake from the tin and serve warm or cool (at room temperature).

BAKER'S TIP

If you don't have any arrowroot, you can use cornflour instead.

Chocolate, Peanut Butter and Banana Cake

Peanut butter and banana is a popular combination with children and adults alike, and the addition of chocolate elevates the flavour even further. Soya flour is rich in protein, so is great for vegan baking and gives the sponge a light texture.

SERVES 8-10

175g/6oz plain white flour
2 tbsp soya flour
50g/1¾oz unsweetened cocoa powder
1 tsp baking powder
1 tsp bicarbonate of soda
2 medium very ripe bananas (approx. 175g/6oz peeled weight)
75g/2¾oz light muscovado or brown soft sugar
150ml/¼ pint rapeseed oil or sunflower oil
150ml/¼ pint plant milk, such almond or hazelnut milk
1 tsp vanilla extract

For the peanut butter frosting:
25g/1oz unsalted plant butter or vegan block margarine, softened
25g/1oz smooth peanut butter
175g/6oz icing sugar, sifted
1½-2 tbsp nut milk, such as almond or hazelnut milk

1   Preheat the oven to 180°C/fan oven 160°C/gas 4. Lightly grease a deep 18cm (7in) round cake tin and line the base with non-stick baking paper.
2   Sift the flours, cocoa powder, baking powder and bicarbonate of soda into a bowl. Peel the bananas and put in a mixing bowl. Mash until smooth. Stir in the sugar. Add the oil, plant milk and vanilla extract and whisk together.

3 Sift the flour mixture over the banana mixture, then working quickly, mix everything together. Spoon and scrape into the prepared tin and level the top.

4 Put the cake in the oven and turn down the temperature to 160°C/fan 140°C/gas 3. Bake for 45 minutes, or until the top is firm and a fine skewer inserted into the centre of the cake comes out clean.

5 Put the cake on a wire rack and leave to cool in the tin for 10 minutes, then carefully turn out onto the wire rack and leave to cool completely. Peel off the baking paper.

6 For the frosting, put the plant butter or margarine and the peanut butter in a bowl and mix together with a wooden spoon. Sift over half the icing sugar and add 1½ tablespoons of the plant milk. Beat together until combined. Sift in the rest of the icing sugar and beat until light and fluffy. Add a little more milk if the icing is too firm. Place the cake on a serving plate and spread the peanut butter icing over the top.

BAKER'S TIP

To make a layered cake, make a double quantity of the peanut frosting. Cut the cake in half horizontally, spread half the frosting over the bottom half of the cake, then top with the other cake. Spread the remaining frosting over the top.

Coffee and Walnut Cake

No teashop or café would be complete without a coffee and walnut cake among its selection and this one is sure to please. The lavish coffee filling and frosting contains dairy-free cream, which gives it a silky richness.

SERVES 8-10

150g/5½oz walnut pieces, roughly chopped
4 tbsp instant coffee powder or granules
2 tbsp near-boiling water
400g/14oz self-raising white flour
2 tsp baking powder
a pinch of salt
250g/9oz light muscovado or light brown soft sugar
400ml/14fl oz plant milk e.g., unsweetened soya or oat milk
100ml/3½fl oz rapeseed oil or sunflower oil
4 tbsp walnut oil

For the filling and frosting:
2 tbsp instant coffee powder or granules
1 tbsp near-boiling water
175g/6oz dairy-free margarine
400g/14oz icing sugar, preferably golden icing sugar, sifted
4 tbsp dairy-free single cream (soya or oat)

1   Put the walnut pieces on a small baking tray in a single layer and place in the cold oven. Preheat to 180°C/fan oven 160°C/gas 4. Cook for 5–7 minutes until very lightly toasted; take care as they burn easily. Remove and leave to cool. Meanwhile, lightly grease two shallow 20cm (8in) or 22cm (8½in) round cake tins and line the bases with non-stick baking paper.

2   Blend the coffee with the hot water in a small bowl and leave to cool. Sift the flour, baking powder and salt into a mixing bowl. Stir in the sugar and two-thirds of the toasted walnuts

and make a hollow in the middle. Mix the plant milk and oils together then add them to the dry ingredients.

3   Quickly mix everything together and divide evenly between the prepared tins. Bake for 18–20 minutes, or until the sponges spring back when gently pressed with a finger and a fine skewer inserted into the middle of the cakes comes out clean.

4   Remove from the oven and put the tins on a wire rack. Leave for 5 minutes, then carefully turn out onto the wire rack and leave to cool. Peel off the baking paper.

5   For the frosting, mix the coffee and hot water in a small bowl and leave to cool. Beat the margarine in a bowl for a few seconds to soften, then gradually mix in the icing sugar, cream and coffee. Beat until light and fluffy.

6   Spread slightly less than half of the frosting over the top of one of the cakes, then top with the second cake. Spread the remaining frosting over the top and scatter over the reserved walnuts.

BAKER'S TIP

Walnut oil enhances the nutty flavour of the sponge, but if you prefer, you can simply use an extra 4 tablespoons of rapeseed or sunflower oil.

Mocha Mayonnaise Cake

Vegan mayonnaise makes an amazing egg substitute and this cake has a lovely rich flavour and slightly squidgy texture – it's a bit like a chocolate brownie. Once baked, you won't be able to detect the mayonnaise in it!

SERVES 8-10

5 tbsp unsweetened cocoa powder
225ml/7½fl oz hot strong-brewed coffee
200g/7oz vegan mayonnaise
225g/8oz soft light brown sugar
275g/9¾oz self-raising white flour
1 tsp baking powder

For the chocolate ganache topping:
100g/3½oz vegan dark chocolate
25g/1oz unsalted plant butter
cake decorations e.g., chocolate coffee beans

1 Preheat the oven to 180°C/fan oven 160°C/gas 4. Lightly grease a 23cm (9in) round cake tin and line the base with non-stick baking paper.

2 Sift the cocoa powder into a bowl and add about a third of the hot coffee. Whisk together until blended. Whisk in a further third of the coffee, then blend in the mayonnaise a spoonful at a time. Stir in the sugar, followed by the rest of the coffee.

3 Sift over the flour and baking powder and quickly and gently fold everything together. Pour and scrape the mixture into the prepared tin.

4 Bake for 35–40 minutes, or until the top is springy when gently pressed and a fine skewer inserted into the middle of the cakes comes out clean. Remove from the oven and place on a wire rack. Leave in the tin for 15 minutes, then turn out onto the wire rack and leave to cool. Peel off the baking paper.

5 For the chocolate ganache topping, break the chocolate into squares and put into a heatproof bowl with the butter. Place the bowl over a pan of near-boiling water. Leave for a few minutes, stirring occasionally until melted and combined. Remove the bowl from the heat and leave to cool for 2 minutes. Pour over the top of the cake and spread to the edges with a palette knife. Decorate as liked; vegan-chocolate-coated coffee beans are perfect.

BAKER'S TIP

Make sure when choosing a vegan mayonnaise for this cake that it is a 'plain' type and not flavoured with ingredients such as lemon or garlic.

Chocolate Truffle Cake

Perfect for a small celebration or family birthday cake, this light chocolate sponge has a simple chocolate buttercream filling and is covered with a rich and glossy chocolate ganache. The covering means the cake can be made a day or two ahead as it will keep the sponge beautifully moist. It looks impressive decorated with homemade or shop-bought small vegan chocolate truffles.

SERVES 6-8

175g/6oz plain flour
40g/1½oz unsweetened cocoa powder
1 tsp baking powder
½ tsp bicarbonate of soda
a pinch of salt (optional)
200g/7oz caster sugar, preferably golden caster sugar
250ml/8½fl oz warm water
75ml/2½fl oz rapeseed oil or sunflower oil
1 tsp vanilla extract
1 tsp cider vinegar

For the chocolate buttercream:
40g/1½oz plant butter or vegan block margarine, softened
75g/2¾oz icing sugar, preferably unrefined, sifted
2 tbsp unsweetened cocoa powder
2 tbsp plant milk e.g., unsweetened soya or almond milk

For the chocolate ganache:
1 tsp plant butter or vegan margarine
4 tbsp plant milk e.g., unsweetened soya or almond milk
150g/5½oz good-quality vegan dark chocolate, broken into pieces
vegan chocolate truffles, to decorate (optional; see Baker's Tip)

1   Preheat the oven to 180°C/fan oven 160°C/gas 4. Lightly grease and line the base and sides of a 10cm- (4in-) deep, 20cm (8in) round cake tin with non-stick baking paper.

2   Sift the flour, cocoa powder, baking powder, bicarbonate of soda and salt (if using) into a large mixing bowl. Stir in the sugar. Stir the water, oil, vanilla extract and cider vinegar together in a jug (they won't mix well, but give them a good whisk), then pour them over the dry ingredients and mix together until smooth.

3   Pour and scrape the mixture into the tin. Bake for 40–45 minutes, or until firm to the touch and a fine skewer inserted into the middle of the cake comes out clean. Put the cake on a wire rack and leave to cool in the tin for 10 minutes, then turn out onto the wire rack and leave to cool. Wrap in cling film (or plastic-free alternative) until ready to fill and decorate (it will be easier to cut if made the day before). Carefully cut the cake in half horizontally with a serrated knife.

4   To make the chocolate buttercream filling, put the plant butter in a bowl and beat for a few seconds with a wooden spoon to soften a little. Sift over the icing sugar and cocoa powder and mix in, then beat until light and fluffy, adding enough of the plant milk to give a soft spreadable consistency. Spread the chocolate buttercream on the bottom cake layer and place the other half on top.

5   For the ganache, put the butter and milk in a small heavy-based saucepan and gently heat until the butter has melted. Remove from the heat, add the chocolate and stir until melted and smooth. Leave to cool until slightly thickened, then pour over the top of the cake and spread over the top and sides using a palette knife. Decorate with chocolate truffles (if using) and leave to set. You can store the cake in a cool place in an airtight container at room temperature for 2–3 days. In

warm weather, store the cake in the fridge (it will lose its glossy appearance when chilled, so let it come to room temperature to regain its shine, before slicing and serving).

BAKER'S TIP

To make vegan chocolate truffles, finely chop 150g/5½oz vegan dark chocolate and put in a heatproof bowl. Put 4 tablespoons of plant milk, 2 teaspoons of caster sugar and 1 teaspoon of vanilla extract in a saucepan and put over a low heat until the sugar dissolves and the milk is steaming hot. Pour over the chocolate, leave for a minute, then stir until smooth. Allow to cool, then chill in the fridge for 3 hours until firm. Roll teaspoons of the mixture into balls, then roll in 2 tablespoons of sifted cocoa powder to coat. Chill until ready to use. (MAKES ABOUT 15)

Chocolate Yule Log

Christmas wouldn't be the same without a Yule log cake, with bark markings all over the chocolate frosting and a pretty dusting of icing sugar 'snow'. Burning a Yule log was a winter solstice ceremony to drive away the short, cold, dark days and this cake is a nod to that tradition.

SERVES 8

240ml/8fl oz plant milk e.g., hazelnut or almond milk
1 tsp cider vinegar
200g/7oz self-raising white flour
2 tbsp unsweetened cocoa powder, plus extra for dusting
½ tsp baking powder
½ tsp bicarbonate of soda
100g/3½oz caster sugar, preferably golden unrefined
60g/2¼oz coconut oil, melted

For the filling:
75g/2¾oz plant butter, softened
150g/5½oz icing sugar
1 tsp unsweetened cocoa powder
2 tsp vanilla extract
2 tsp plant milk

For the chocolate frosting:
50g/1¾oz vegan dark chocolate, roughly chopped
100g/3½oz plant butter or vegan block margarine
100g/3½oz icing sugar, sifted, plus extra for dusting
1 tbsp unsweetened cocoa powder, sifted
1 tsp vanilla extract

1   Preheat the oven to 180°C/fan oven 160°C/gas 4. Grease a 30 x 24cm (12 x 9½in) Swiss roll tin and line the base with non-stick baking paper. Pour the plant milk into a jug, add the

vinegar and stir well. Leave to stand for 5–10 minutes; the mixture will thicken and have a slightly curdled appearance.

2   Sift the flour, cocoa powder, baking powder and bicarbonate of soda into a bowl. Add the caster sugar and stir well, then make a hollow in the middle. Add the melted coconut oil to the milk, whisk for a few seconds, then add to the dry ingredients. Mix everything together until just combined. Pour and scrape the mixture into the prepared tin, spreading it out to the corners if necessary. Tap the tin on the work surface to remove any air bubbles.

3   Bake for 16–18 minutes, or until the sponge is springy to the touch and a fine skewer inserted into the middle of the sponge comes out clean. Lay a large piece of non-stick baking paper on the work surface and dust it with cocoa powder. Turn out the sponge, peel off the baking paper used to line the tin, then trim the edges of the sponge with a sharp knife. Roll up the sponge tightly from one of the longer edges with the paper inside. Cover with a damp clean tea towel and leave to cool.

4   While the sponge is cooling, make the filling. Put the plant butter in a bowl and beat for a few seconds. Sift over the icing sugar and cocoa powder and mix into the butter. Add the vanilla and plant milk, then beat until light and fluffy. Unroll the sponge and spread the filling evenly over the sponge, then re-roll tightly without the baking paper inside.

5   For the chocolate frosting, put the chocolate in a heatproof bowl over a pan of very hot water. Leave for a few minutes, stirring occasionally until the chocolate has melted, then remove the bowl from the heat.

6   Beat the plant butter in a bowl until soft and creamy. Beat in the icing sugar, cocoa powder and vanilla extract, then add the melted chocolate and beat until light and fluffy. Spread over the roulade, then use a fork or thin spatula to create a bark-

like pattern. Dust with icing sugar. Store in an airtight container in the fridge until ready to serve and eat within a few days of making.

Red Velvet Cake

This red-coloured sponge cake is very popular, particularly with those who don't like their chocolate cake to be dark and rich. Definitely a cake for those with a sweet tooth, it has a subtle chocolate flavour and beautiful colour.

SERVES 10-12

400g/14oz self-raising white flour
15g/½oz unsweetened cocoa powder
2 tsp baking powder
¼ tsp salt
240g/8½oz caster sugar
1½ tsp red food colouring gel or paste (not liquid)
200ml/7fl oz plant milk e.g., unsweetened soya or oat milk
200ml/7fl oz unsweetened vegan yogurt e.g., coconut or soya yogurt
150ml/¼ pint rapeseed oil or sunflower oil
1 tbsp vanilla extract

For the cream cheese frosting:
200g/7oz plant butter or vegan block margarine, softened
375g/13oz icing sugar, sifted
1 tsp vanilla extract
160g/5½oz full-fat vegan cream cheese, at room temperature

1 Preheat the oven to 180°C/fan oven 160°C/gas 4. Lightly grease three shallow 20cm (8in) or 22cm (8½in) round cake tins and line the bases with non-stick baking paper.
2 Sift the flour, cocoa powder, baking powder and salt into a bowl. Add the sugar and stir to mix, then make a hollow in the middle.
3 Blend the red food colouring with 1 tablespoon of the milk, then whisk in the rest of the milk until the milk is an even red colour. Stir in the yogurt, then add the oil and vanilla extract

and whisk for a few seconds. Add to the dry ingredients and quickly mix until just combined.

4   Divide the mixture evenly among the prepared tins. Tap each tin a couple of times on the work surface, then bake for 18–20 minutes, or until a fine skewer inserted into the middle of each sponge comes out clean. Put the cakes on wire racks and leave to cool in the tins for 5 minutes, then carefully turn out onto the wire racks and leave until completely cool. Wrap each cake in cling film (or plastic-free alternative) and leave overnight (the cakes will become moister).

5   The following day, make the frosting. Put the plant butter or margarine in a mixing bowl and sift over the icing sugar. Add the vanilla extract, mix together, then beat with a wooden spoon until creamy. Gently beat the vegan cream cheese to soften, then gently stir into the butter and sugar mixture.

6   Sandwich the three sponge cakes together with the cream cheese frosting. Spread the rest of the over the top and sides give it a swirl with the knife. Store the cake in an airtight container and keep in the fridge until ready to serve. Eat within 5 days.

BAKER'S TIP

If you don't have three tins, you can divide the mixture between two 22-23cm (8½-9in) cake tins. As the sponges will be deeper, you will need to cook them for 20-25 minutes.

Sachertorte

Created by a 16-year-old apprentice chef Franz Sacher in 1832, the original recipe for this dense rich chocolate cake is a well-kept secret. Most non-vegan versions contain at least half a dozen eggs, but this vegan version – obviously egg-free – matches them all in flavour and texture.

SERVES 10

175g/6oz vegan dark chocolate, broken into squares
200g/7oz golden caster sugar
200g/7oz soft non-dairy margarine, at room temperature
2 tsp vanilla extract
250g/9oz plain white flour
25g/1oz cornflour
1 tbsp baking powder
a pinch of salt
150ml/¼ pint cold brewed coffee
2 tsp cider vinegar
150g/5½oz apricot jam, warmed and sieved

For the chocolate ganache icing:
200g/7oz vegan dark chocolate, broken into squares
85g/3oz plant butter or vegan block margarine

1 Preheat the oven to 180°C/fan oven 160°C/gas 4. Lightly grease a deep 22cm (8½in) round cake tin and line the base with non-stick baking paper.
2 Put the chocolate squares in a heatproof bowl. Place over a pan of very hot water and leave for a few minutes, stirring occasionally until melted. Remove the bowl from the heat and leave until just cool. Alternatively, melt the chocolate in the microwave (blast for 20 seconds at a time, then stir to prevent hot-spots which may burn).
3 Put the golden caster sugar, soft margarine and vanilla extract in a bowl and mix together, then beat until light and fluffy. Gradually beat in the melted chocolate.
4 Sift the flour, cornflour, baking powder and salt into a bowl and mix well, then sift again over the chocolate mixture. Stir

the coffee and vinegar together and add to the bowl, then gently fold everything together.

5   Pour and scrape the mixture into the prepared cake tin. Bake for 50–55 minutes, or until a fine skewer inserted into the middle of the cake comes out clean. Turn off the oven and leave the cake to cool inside with the door ajar for 30 minutes. Remove and leave on a wire rack to cool for a further 10 minutes before turning out. Cover the cake with a sheet of foil or with a tea towel and leave until cold.

6   Using a large serrated knife, cut the cake in half horizontally. Spread 75g/2¾oz of the jam over the cut side of the bottom sponge, then replace the other half to sandwich them back together. Spread the remaining jam over the top of the cake.

7   For the icing, put the chocolate squares in a heatproof bowl with the plant butter. Place over a pan of very hot water and leave for a few minutes, stirring occasionally until melted and blended. Alternatively, melt the chocolate in the microwave (blast for 20 seconds at a time, then stir to prevent hot-spots which may burn). Leave to cool for a few minutes so that it thickens slightly, then pour and spread evenly over the top and sides of the cake. Leave to cool and set before serving. Store in an airtight container for up to 5 days.

BAKER'S TIPS

Sachertorte has a wonderfully moist dense texture and during baking the cake may dip very slightly in the middle. This can easily be rectified when you ice the cake, by spreading a little more jam and icing in the centre.

The word 'Sacher' is traditionally piped on the top of the cake in milk chocolate. If you wish, melt 25g/1oz vegan milk chocolate in a heatproof bowl over hot water (or in the microwave in short bursts). Spoon into a greaseproof-paper piping bag, snip off the tip and write 'Sacher' on the cake.

Bermuda Banana Bread

My mother grew up in Bermuda where bananas grew in the backyard. This was her favourite cake, which she made whenever there were a few very ripe bananas left in the fruit bowl. She always insisted on the prefix 'Bermuda' even when she moved to England in the 1950s. While her original recipe was made with butter, I find that coconut oil works even better and adds a subtle tropical flavour to the mix.

MAKES 8-10 SLICES

65g/2½oz coconut oil, melted, plus extra for greasing
75g/2¾oz pecans, roughly chopped
4 small or 3 medium very ripe bananas (about 250g/9oz peeled weight)
100g/3½oz light brown soft sugar
40g/1½oz ground almonds
4 tbsp coconut 'drink' milk or other plant milk
1 tsp lemon juice
250g/9oz self-raising white flour
1 tsp baking powder
½ tsp bicarbonate of soda

1 Lightly grease a 900g (2lb) loaf tin with melted coconut oil and line the base with non-stick baking paper. Put the pecans on a baking tray and put into a cold oven. Turn the oven on to 180°C/fan oven 160°C/gas 4. Roast the nuts for 5–7 minutes until they smell nutty and are just started to darken. Take care not to let them burn. Remove from the oven.

2 While the nuts are roasting, mash the bananas in a mixing bowl until fairly smooth (a few small lumps are fine). Stir in the melted coconut oil, followed by the sugar and ground almonds. Mix the milk and lemon juice together.

3 Sift the flour, baking powder and bicarbonate of soda over the mashed bananas and melted coconut oil. Add the pecans and

start folding into the mixture. When it is half-mixed, add the milk and lemon juice blend and, working quickly, continue to fold everything together.

4   Spoon and scrape the mixture into the prepared tin. Bake for about 50 minutes, or until a fine skewer inserted into the middle of the cake comes out clean. Cover the top with foil if it starts to brown too much.

5   Put the cake on a wire rack and leave to cool in the tin for 15 minutes, then turn out onto the wire rack, peeling off the baking paper. Leave to cool. Serve thickly sliced, thinly spread with a little plant butter or margarine, if liked.

BAKER'S TIP

Make sure that the bananas are really ripe for the best flavour and texture; the skins should be at least half black and the bananas soft when gently squeezed.

VARIATION

For banana and coconut bread, add 2 tablespoons of lightly toasted desiccated coconut instead of the pecans.

Sticky Gingerbread

Prunes may seem an unusual addition to gingerbread, but when finely chopped they seem to 'melt' into the mixture and make an excellent egg alternative. This gingerbread rivals any non-vegan version and becomes richer and stickier after keeping for a few days, well wrapped or stored in an airtight tin.

SERVES 12

100g/3½oz ready-to-eat soft prunes (about 12), finely chopped
2 tbsp boiling water
250ml/8½fl oz plant milk e.g., unsweetened soya or oat milk
2 tsp cider vinegar
250ml/8½fl oz golden syrup
150ml/¼ pint black treacle
150ml/¼ pint rapeseed oil or sunflower oil
120g/4oz dark muscovado or brown soft sugar
300g/10½oz plain white flour
1 tbsp ground ginger
2 tsp ground cinnamon
1 tsp ground allspice
1 tsp bicarbonate of soda
a pinch of salt

1 Put the chopped prunes in a heavy-based saucepan and spoon over the boiling water. Stir and leave to stand for a few minutes. Pour the milk into a jug and stir in the vinegar. Set aside. Lightly grease a 23cm (9in) square cake tin and line the base with a square of non-stick baking paper. Preheat the oven to 170°C/fan oven 150°C/gas 3.

2 Add the golden syrup, treacle, oil and sugar to the prunes. Warm the mixture over a low heat until the sugar has completely dissolved, stirring occasionally until combined. Turn off the heat.

3   Sift the flour, ginger, cinnamon, allspice, bicarbonate of soda and salt into a large bowl. Make a hollow in the middle.

4   Add the melted mixture to the flour with the milk. Working quickly (as the bicarbonate of soda will be activated), stir everything together until combined. Pour and scrape the mixture into the prepared tin.

5   Bake for 45 minutes, or until the cake is firm and feels springy when the top is gently touched.

6   Put the cake on a wire rack and leave to cool in the tin for about 30 minutes, then remove (leaving the baking paper in place) and leave to cool completely on the wire rack. Wrap in foil. Leave the gingerbread to mature for at least 2 days before slicing; it will keep for up to 10 days, wrapped in foil or stored in an airtight tin.

BAKER'S TIP

Like traditional gingerbread, this cake improves by keeping for a few days before eating. The flavours mellow and mature and the texture becomes softer and stickier.

Spiced Butternut Squash Teabread

Vegetable puree such as butternut squash makes an excellent egg and fat substitute and adds sweetness and a vibrant colour to this spicy teabread. Here, the squash is steam-boiled to retain all the flavour and nutrients.

SERVES 8

300g/10½oz peeled butternut squash, diced
150g/5½oz agave syrup
75g/2¾oz ready-to-eat apricots, chopped
200g/7oz self-raising white flour
100g/3½oz self-raising wholemeal flour
1 tsp ground cinnamon
1 tsp ground ginger
¼ tsp finely grated nutmeg
150g/5½oz cold plant butter or vegan block margarine, diced
2 tbsp pumpkin seeds

1 Preheat the oven to 180°C/fan oven 160°C/gas 4. Lightly grease a 900g (2lb) loaf tin and line the base with non-stick baking paper.
2 Put the butternut squash in a heavy-based saucepan with 4 tablespoons of water. Bring to the boil, cover the pan with a lid, then lower the heat and let the squash steam for 10–12 minutes, or until tender when pierced with a sharp knife. Tip into a sieve and drain thoroughly, then return to the pan and mash until smooth. Stir in the agave syrup and dried apricots. Leave uncovered to cool for a few minutes.
3 Sift the flours and spices into a mixing bowl, tipping in the bran left in the sieve. Add the butter and rub in with your fingertips until the mixture resembles breadcrumbs. Stir in the pumpkin seeds.

4 Add the butternut squash mixture to the bowl and stir together until combined. Spoon and scrape into the prepared tin and smooth the surface level. Bake for 45–50 minutes, or until well risen, lightly browned and firm.

5 Allow the loaf to cool in the tin on a wire rack for 10 minutes, then turn out onto the wire rack and peel off the baking paper. Serve in slices when the loaf is barely warm or leave until cold. Store in an airtight tin and eat within 2 days of making.

BAKER'S TIP

This is a great way to use up the flesh from scooped-out pumpkins at Halloween. Cook in exactly the same way as butternut squash.

Castagnaccio

A classic Tuscan dessert cake, Castagnaccio is not a light airy
sponge, but a shallow, fairly dense bake enriched with olive oil and
the flavour of nutty chestnut flour and enhanced with aromatic
orange zest and fresh rosemary. The top is always scattered with
pine nuts and usually includes hazelnuts or walnuts, as used here.

SERVES 8-10

1 medium orange, preferably unwaxed
75g/2¾oz sultanas or raisins
300g/10½oz chestnut flour
a pinch of salt
4 tbsp olive oil, plus extra for greasing
450–500ml/1 pint–17fl oz sweetened rice milk
2 tsp vanilla extract
1 tsp chopped fresh rosemary leaves, plus optional fresh
   sprigs to decorate
75g/2¾oz pine nuts
75g/2¾oz walnuts, roughly chopped
dandelion 'honey' (see Baker's Tip) or agave syrup, to serve

1   Finely grate the zest of the orange and set aside, then halve and
    squeeze out the juice. Put the sultanas or raisins in a small bowl
    and add the orange juice. Leave to soak for at least 1 hour,
    preferably overnight in the fridge, so that they plump up.
2   Preheat the oven to 200°C/fan oven 180°C/gas 6. Lightly oil a
    23–25cm (9–10in) loose-bottomed round tin (the larger size
    is better if you have a choice of tins) and line the base with a
    circle of non-stick baking paper.
3   Sift the flour and salt into a bowl and make a hollow in the
    middle. Add the orange zest, 2 tablespoons of the oil, the
    vanilla extract and rosemary to 450ml/1 pint of the milk, then
    add to the dry ingredients. Gradually work the flour into the
    milk with a whisk to make a smooth soft batter; it should be
    thin enough to fall from the whisk, if not add a little more
    milk. Drain the raisins and stir them into the mixture.

4 Spoon and scrape the mixture into the prepared tin. Put the nuts in a bowl and drizzle over the remaining 2 tablespoons of oil. Toss to coat, then scatter evenly over the top of the cake. Bake for 30–35 minutes, or until a thin, slightly cracked crust has formed on top; the inside should still be soft. Check after about 20 minutes baking; if the nuts start to brown too much, cover the top with foil.

5 Leave the cake to cool in the tin, then remove, peel off the baking paper and put on a serving plate. Garnish with some sprigs of fresh rosemary, if liked. Serve cut into wedges and drizzled with dandelion honey or agave syrup. Keep the cake covered with a clean tea towel for up to 4 days at room temperature. In warm weather, cover with cling film (or plastic-free alternative) and keep in the fridge. Do not freeze or the texture will become rubbery.

BAKER'S TIP

To make dandelion 'honey': Rinse 100g/3½oz fresh dandelion flowerheads in cold water to remove any dust or bugs. Put in a saucepan with 2 slices of lemon and pour over 300ml/½ pint water. Slowly bring to the boil, then cover the pan with a lid and simmer for 12 minutes. Turn off the heat and leave for at least 6 hours or overnight to steep. Strain the liquid, squeezing out the flowers to extract as much flavour as possible. Measure and return to the cleaned pan with an equal amount of sugar e.g., if there is 250ml/8½fl oz liquid, add 250g/9oz caster or granulated sugar. Slowly bring to the boil, stirring until the sugar has dissolved, then simmer for 20-30 minutes until syrupy; it will thicken further on cooling. Pour into clean sterilised jars and store for up to 3 months. Remember when picking dandelions that they are important for pollinators, so always pick from a clean and plentiful place (avoid busy roads and dog-walking routes) and leave a few flowers in every patch.

CHAPTER TWO

Small Cakes, Muffins and Brownies

....

For accompaniments to mid-morning coffee at home or the office, afternoon tea with friends, to tuck into lunchboxes or pack in picnic baskets, small individual bakes are often more versatile than large ones. From all manner of little sponge cupcakes with rich, silky frostings to moist berry muffins and squidgy indulgent brownies, you'll find lots of mini treats here. Not everyone has a sweet tooth, of course, and for those who prefer savouries, try baking a batch of Mushroom and Pine Nut Muffins or Sweet Potato and Herb Muffins.

These are bakes that truly test your willpower not to eat more than one in a single sitting. If you can't resist temptation, make sure you pack some away in freezer-proof boxes – wrap them separately – and freeze for another day.

Vanilla Cupcakes

Sometimes a simple flavouring like vanilla is the best and these light little sponges are delicious topped with a generous swirl of creamy frosting and a scattering of sugar sprinkles.

MAKES 12

200ml/7fl oz plant milk e.g., almond or unsweetened soya milk
4 tsp cider vinegar
200g/7oz self-raising white flour
¼ tsp baking powder
¼ tsp bicarbonate of soda
a pinch of salt (optional)
180g/6oz caster sugar
5 tbsp rapeseed oil or sunflower oil
1 tbsp vanilla extract

For the vanilla frosting:
40g/1½oz dairy-free soft margarine
40g/1½oz white solid vegetable fat
1 tbsp vanilla extract
200g/7oz icing sugar
1 tbsp plant milk e.g., almond or unsweetened soya milk
vegan sugar sprinkles (optional)

1   Preheat the oven to 180°C/fan oven 160°C/gas 4. Line a muffin tin with 12 cupcake cases. In a small jug or bowl mix the plant milk and cider vinegar. Leave for 5 minutes.
2   Meanwhile, sift the flour, baking powder, bicarbonate of soda and salt (if using) into a mixing bowl. Stir in the sugar. Add the oil and vanilla extract to the milk. Make a hollow in the middle of the dry ingredients, then add the milk mixture. Quickly mix everything together until just combined; the batter should still be a bit lumpy.
3   Divide the mixture evenly among the cupcake cases, then tap the tray on the work surface a couple of times to pop any

bubbles and stop the raising agents acting too quickly. Bake for 15 minutes until the sponges are well risen and springy and firm to the touch.

4 Place the muffin tin on a wire rack and leave for 15 minutes, then remove the cupcakes from the tin and leave to cool on the rack.

5 For the frosting, put the margarine and vegetable fat in a mixing bowl and, using an electric or hand-held whisk or wooden spoon, beat until soft and creamy. Add the vanilla extract and sift over half the icing sugar. Mix together, then sift over the remaining icing sugar, beat in, then continue beating for a minute or two until light and fluffy. Spread or pipe the frosting over the top of each cupcake and decorate with vegan sugar sprinkles or as you like. Store in an airtight container and keep at room temperature for up to 2 days or in the fridge for up to 4 days. These can also be frozen.

BAKER'S TIP

Making the frosting with a combination of dairy-free margarine and white vegetable fat makes it light in both colour and texture, so make sure you choose a pale-coloured margarine. This is a great frosting if you want to colour it, in pastel or rainbow shades, for example.

Chocolate and Cherry Cupcakes

These little cakes have a generous flat-iced fudgy topping so use deep cupcake cases and don't overfill them with cake mixture; the risen sponges should come no further than halfway up the cases. Here, five cakes have a chocolate topping and five a cherry topping, but you can make all chocolate or all cherry if you prefer by doubling your chosen topping.

MAKES 10

100ml/3½fl oz plant milk e.g., unsweetened soya milk or oat milk
2 tsp cider vinegar
75g/2¾oz self-raising white flour
15g/½oz unsweetened cocoa powder
a pinch of salt (optional)
90g/3oz caster sugar
3 tbsp rapeseed oil or sunflower oil
2 tsp vanilla extract

For the chocolate topping:
50g/1¾oz vegan dark chocolate, broken into squares
20g/¾oz plant butter or vegan block margarine
20g/¾oz icing sugar

For the cherry topping:
100g/3½oz icing sugar
1 tbsp boiling water
1½ tsp plant butter or vegan block margarine
1 tsp cherry syrup from a jar of maraschino cherries
5 maraschino cherries

1 Preheat the oven to 180°C/fan oven 160°C/gas 4. Line a muffin tin with 10 cupcake cases. In a small jug or bowl mix the plant milk and cider vinegar. Leave for 5 minutes.
2 Meanwhile, sift the flour, cocoa powder and salt (if using) into a mixing bowl. Stir in the sugar and make a hollow in the middle. Add the oil and vanilla to the milk mixture, stir (it won't

completely mix together), then add to the dry ingredients. Quickly mix everything together until just combined; the batter should still be a bit lumpy.

3 Divide the mixture evenly among the cupcake cases, then tap the tray on the work surface a couple of times to pop any bubbles and stop the raising agents acting too quickly. Bake for 15 minutes until the sponges are just cooked and springy. A fine skewer inserted into the middle of a cake should come out clean.

4 Place the muffin tin on a wire rack and leave for 15 minutes, then remove the cupcakes and leave to cool on the rack.

5 For the chocolate topping, break the chocolate into squares and put in a heatproof bowl with the plant butter over a pan of very hot water. Leave until melted, stirring occasionally, then remove the bowl and leave to cool for about a minute. Sift over the icing sugar and stir until blended. Immediately spoon the chocolate topping over five of the cupcakes.

6 For the cherry topping, sift the icing sugar into a bowl. Put the water and plant butter into a small bowl or jug and microwave for about 10 seconds, or until the butter has melted. Add to the icing sugar with the cherry syrup, then mix together to make a smooth icing. Spoon over the tops of the remaining five cupcakes and finish each with a maraschino cherry. Leave the iced cakes to set. Store in an airtight container (in the fridge if the weather is warm) and eat within 3 days.

BAKER'S TIP

You can use the warmth of the turned-off oven to melt the mixture for the toppings if liked, but make sure you use heatproof bowls.

VARIATION

Instead of giving the cupcakes a flat-topped icing, you could make a fluffy vanilla frosting (page 84) and decorate with shavings of vegan chocolate.

Chocolate Hazelnut Cupcakes

Demerara sugar give these cupcakes a hint of caramel flavour which works well with the chocolate and hazelnuts. Because of the large crystals the sugar is gently dissolved first in the milk and oil; as the cake batter is already warm, the cupcakes will take a little less time to cook.

MAKES 12

175ml/6fl oz hazelnut milk
2 tsp cider vinegar
4 tbsp rapeseed oil or sunflower oil
100g/3½oz demerara sugar
175g/6oz self-raising white flour
30g/1oz unsweetened cocoa powder
a pinch of salt
½ tsp bicarbonate of soda

For the frosting:
40g/1½oz plant butter or vegan block margarine, softened
100g/3½oz icing sugar, sifted
50g/1¾oz vegan chocolate hazelnut spread (see Baker's Tip)
1 tsp vanilla extract
50g/1¾oz chopped toasted hazelnuts or whole hazelnuts, to decorate

1 Preheat the oven to 180°C/fan oven 160°C/gas 4. Line a muffin tin with 12 cupcake cases. Put the hazelnut milk, vinegar, oil and sugar in a small heavy-based saucepan and gently heat for 3–4 minutes, stirring frequently until the sugar has dissolved. Remove from the heat and leave to cool for 4 minutes.

2 Sift the flour, cocoa powder, salt and bicarbonate of soda into a bowl. Make a hollow in the middle, then pour in the milk and sugar mixture. Quickly stir everything together until just combined; it should still look slightly lumpy.

3 Divide evenly among the cupcake cases, then tap the tray on the work surface a couple of times to pop any bubbles and stop the raising agents acting too quickly. Bake for 15–18 minutes, or until firm; the tops should feel springy to the touch and a fine skewer inserted into the middle of a cake should come out clean.

4 Allow the cupcakes to cool in the tin on a wire rack for 5 minutes, then remove and cool on the wire rack.

5 For the frosting, beat the plant butter or margarine in a bowl until creamy, then gradually work in the icing sugar. Beat for a few minutes until light and fluffy. Add the hazelnut spread and vanilla extract and beat until just mixed. Spoon or pipe the frosting onto the cakes and decorate with chopped or whole hazelnuts. Store in an airtight container (in the fridge if the weather is warm) and eat within 3 days.

BAKER'S TIP

You can buy vegan chocolate hazelnut spread or make your own if you have a powerful food processor. Put 250g/9oz skinned hazelnuts in a non-stick frying pan and cook over a low heat for 5–6 minutes, shaking the pan frequently, until the nuts are lightly browned (watch carefully as they burn easily). While they are still hot, tip into a food processor and blend for 4–5 minutes until the nuts are blended to a thick creamy paste. Melt 100g/3½oz chopped vegan dark chocolate in a small heatproof bowl over a pan of very hot water or in the microwave (blast for 20 seconds at a time, then stir to prevent hot-spots which may burn). Add the melted chocolate to the nut paste and blend for a few seconds to combine. Sift over 100g/3½oz icing sugar and 3 tablespoons of unsweetened cocoa powder and blend again. Spoon and scrape into a clean jar, seal with a lid and store in the fridge. It will keep for up to a month.

Chocolate Party Traybake

Perfect for parties or entertaining, this chocolate sponge is baked in a rectangular tin and can be cut into small squares or rectangles to feed a crowd. Top simply with vegan sugar sprinkles, or with candles and decorations to match the occasion.

SERVES 15-20

300ml/½ pint plant milk e.g., unsweetened soya or oat milk
2 tsp cider vinegar
325g/11¼oz light muscovado or light brown soft sugar
2 tsp vanilla extract
200ml/7fl oz rapeseed or sunflower oil, plus extra for greasing
175g/6oz vegan yogurt e.g., soya or coconut yogurt
325g/11¼oz self-raising white flour
75g/2¾oz unsweetened cocoa powder
1 tsp baking powder
1 tsp bicarbonate of soda
a pinch of salt

For the chocolate frosting:
100g/3½oz vegan dark chocolate, broken into squares
150g/5½oz dairy-free spread, softened
1 tsp vanilla extract
300g/10½oz icing sugar, preferably unrefined, sifted
vegan sugar sprinkles, to decorate

1   Preheat the oven to 180°C/fan oven 160°C/gas 4. Lightly grease a 33 x 23cm (13 x 9in) cake tin, at least 4cm (1½in) deep, and line the base with non-stick baking paper. Pour the milk into a jug, add the vinegar and whisk together with a fork. Leave for a few minutes; the mixture will curdle.

2   Put the sugar, vanilla extract and oil in a bowl and whisk together with a hand-held or electric whisk, making sure to break down any lumps in the sugar. Whisk in the yogurt, followed by the milk mixture.

3 Sift the flour, cocoa powder, baking powder, bicarbonate of soda and salt into a bowl to mix together, then sift again, this time over the wet ingredients. Quickly mix together until just combined, then pour and scrape the mixture into the prepared tin.

4 Bake for 30–35 minutes, or until well risen, springy to the touch and a fine skewer inserted into the middle comes out fairly clean. Put the cake on a wire rack and leave to cool in the tin for 20 minutes, then carefully turn out onto the wire rack and leave to cool completely. Peel off the baking paper.

5 For the frosting: Put the squares of chocolate in a heatproof bowl over a pan of very hot water. Leave for a few minutes, stirring occasionally, until melted. Remove from the heat and allow to cool for 5 minutes. Alternatively, melt the chocolate in the microwave (blast for 20 seconds at a time, then stir to prevent hot-spots which may burn).

6 Meanwhile, put the dairy-free spread in a bowl with the vanilla extract. Sift over the icing sugar and gradually mix in the icing sugar, then beat until light and fluffy. Add the cooled melted chocolate and beat again. If the frosting is a little soft, chill in the fridge for 10–20 minutes before using.

7 Spread the frosting over the top of the cake and decorate with sugar sprinkles. Put the cake in the fridge for an hour, then cover with cling film (or plastic-free alternative) to stop the sponge from drying out. Store in the fridge and remove about an hour before serving to allow it to soften. Eat within 3 days of making.

VARIATION

For a chocolate orange traybake, leave out the vanilla extract in both the sponge and the frosting. Add the finely grated zest of 1 orange (preferably unwaxed) to the sponge and the finely grated zest of ½ orange to the frosting.

Lemon Magdalenas

The word 'magdalenas' simply means 'cupcake' in Spanish and these little lemon cakes are naturally vegan as they are always made with olive oil (never butter). Flavoured with lemon zest, they are popular at breakfast time where they are served warm from the oven with milky coffee ('café con leche'). Traditionally they were baked in metal shell-shaped moulds, but today they are usually made in cupcake cases.

MAKES 12

200ml/7fl oz plant milk e.g., almond milk
100ml/3½fl oz mild olive oil
150g/5½oz caster sugar
finely grated zest of 1 large lemon, preferably unwaxed
a small pinch of salt (optional)
200g/7oz self-raising white flour
1 tsp baking powder

1   Preheat the oven to 180°C/fan oven 160°C/gas 4. Grease a 12-hole non-stick muffin tin or line it with 12 paper cupcake cases.
2   Put the plant milk, olive oil, sugar, lemon zest and salt (if using) in a bowl and beat with a hand-held or electric whisk until combined. Sift over the flour and baking powder and quickly beat into the wet ingredients until just mixed.
3   Divide the mixture equally among the paper cases or greased holes in the muffin tin so that they are about three-quarters full. Bake for about 18 minutes, or until well risen, golden brown and slightly springy to the touch.
4   Leave in the tins on a wire rack for 5 minutes, then transfer to the wire rack. Serve warm or cool. Store in an airtight container at room temperature and eat within 4 days of making.

VARIATIONS

Every bakery and café in Spain has its own recipe for these and you can alter yours to suit your own preferences. For a sugary crust, sprinkle the tops with a little caster or demerara sugar before baking. Other popular variations include adding a teaspoon or two of vanilla extract (it works surprisingly well with the lemon), adding orange zest as well as lemon, or using a fruity olive oil rather than a light mild one (but make sure you are a big olive oil fan before going with this one as the taste is quite distinctive).

Blueberry Muffins

These gluten-free muffins are packed with juicy blueberries and are excellent to serve for a brunch or mid-morning snack. Unlike most muffins, the flavour and texture improves when they are left overnight as the berry juice soaks into the sponge.

MAKES 6

100g/3½oz chickpea flour or besan (gram) flour
25g/1oz oat flour (page 11)
50g/1¾oz ground almonds
¾ tsp baking powder
½ tsp bicarbonate of soda
150–200g/5½–7oz fresh blueberries
120ml/4fl oz unsweetened soya or oat milk
5 tbsp maple syrup or maple and carob syrup blend
45g/1½oz (3 tbsp) apple puree (page 12)
1 tsp vanilla extract
1 tsp lemon juice

1   Preheat the oven to 200°C/fan oven 180°C/gas 6. Grease 6 holes in a non-stick 12-hole muffin tin or line it with 6 paper muffin cases.
2   Put the chickpea flour, oat flour, ground almonds, baking powder and bicarbonate of soda into a mixing bowl and stir together until well mixed. Stir in the blueberries. Make a hollow in the middle of the mixture.
3   Mix together the milk, maple syrup, apple puree and vanilla extract in a bowl or jug. Add the wet ingredients to the dry ingredients and stir briefly until just combined; the mixture should still look very lumpy.
4   Spoon or ladle the batter into the prepared muffin tin, dividing it evenly among the muffin holes or cupcake cases. Put into the oven, then immediately lower the temperature to

190°C/fan oven 170°C/gas 5. Bake for 16–18 minutes, or until golden brown, well risen and firm to the touch.

5 Cool in the tin for 5 minutes, then remove the muffins from the tin and leave to cool on a wire rack. Once completely cool, store in an airtight container at room temperature for at least 6 hours before serving. Eat within 3 days of making, storing in the fridge after 24 hours.

VARIATION

For raspberry and lemon muffins, use fresh raspberries instead of blueberries and add the finely grated zest of 1 lemon with the liquid ingredients. Use an extra 1 teaspoon of plant milk instead of the vanilla extract.

Chocolate and Coconut Muffins

Creamed coconut not only adds a rich flavour to these muffins but makes them beautifully moist too. For a more distinctive coconut taste, dissolve the creamed coconut in 150ml/¼ pint boiling water, then stir in 150ml/¼ pint coconut 'drink' milk.

MAKES 9

300ml/½ pint boiling water
50g/1¾oz creamed coconut (in a solid block), chopped
6 tbsp coconut oil, rapeseed oil or sunflower oil
225g/8oz self-raising white flour
25g/1oz unsweetened cocoa powder, plus ½ tsp for dusting
1 tsp baking powder
a pinch of salt (optional)
90g/3oz light muscovado or light brown soft sugar
1 tsp icing sugar, preferably golden icing sugar

1 Preheat the oven to 190°C/fan oven 170°C/gas 5. Grease 9 holes of a 12-hole non-stick muffin tin or line it with 9 paper muffin cases.

2 Pour the boiling water into a heatproof jug, add the chopped creamed coconut and stir until completely dissolved. Add the oil and set aside until barely warm (if using coconut oil, it will melt in the heat).

3 Sift the flour, cocoa powder, baking powder and salt (if using) into a bowl. Add the sugar and stir until well mixed. Add the wet ingredients to the dry ingredients and stir briefly, using a rubber spatula or spoon to gently combine and moisten the dry ingredients. Stop mixing while the batter is still lumpy; the lumps will disappear when the muffins are baked.

4 Spoon or ladle the batter into the prepared muffin tin, dividing it evenly among the holes or cases. Put into the oven, then immediately lower the temperature to 180°C/fan oven

160°C/gas 4. Bake for 15–18 minutes, or until well risen and firm to the touch.

5 Cool in the tin for 5 minutes, then remove the muffins from the tin and leave to cool on a wire rack. Dust the tops of the muffins with sifted icing sugar, then with cocoa powder. Serve warm or cold. Store the muffins in an airtight container as soon as they are cool. Although they are best eaten fresh on the day of making, they will keep for a day or two. They can be frozen for up to 3 months and will take around 30 minutes to thaw at room temperature or just a few seconds in the microwave.

BAKER'S TIP

Once the batter is mixed, the baking agent has been activated, so you need to get the muffins into the oven as soon as possible: work quickly to fill the muffin cases or muffin holes.

VARIATIONS

For chocolate and orange muffins, add the finely grated zest of 1 orange (preferably unwaxed) to the wet ingredients. You could also add 75g/2¾oz roughly chopped orange-flavoured vegan chocolate when stirring the sugar into the dry ingredients.

Instead of dusting with icing sugar and cocoa after baking, you could give the muffins a crunchy sugar topping. Sprinkle the muffins with coarse sugar before baking.

For a streusel topping (make this before you start making the muffins), rub 35g/1¼oz cold plant butter or vegan block margarine into 50g/1¾oz plain flour until the mixture resembles breadcrumbs. Stir in 2 tablespoons of light brown soft sugar or caster sugar, then gently squeeze into a ball. Wrap and chill for at least 20 minutes, then coarsely grate before sprinkling over the muffin batter in the tin just before baking.

Mushroom and Pine Nut Muffins

Muffins don't have to be sweet and sugary. These savoury ones are packed with tender mushrooms and crunchy toasted pine nuts. The fresh rosemary gives them a hint of Mediterranean flavour.

MAKES 7 LARGE MUFFINS

1 tbsp cider vinegar
120ml/4fl oz plant milk e.g., unsweetened soya or oat milk
75g/2¾oz pine nuts
2 tbsp rapeseed oil or sunflower oil
175g/6oz button mushrooms, cleaned and sliced
150g/5½oz plain white flour
100g/3½oz plain wholemeal flour
2½ tsp baking powder
1 tsp bicarbonate of soda
a pinch of salt
1 tbsp nutritional yeast
1 tsp finely chopped fresh rosemary leaves
75g/2¾oz plant butter or dairy-free margarine, melted

1   Preheat the oven to 190°C/fan oven 170°C/gas 5. Lightly grease 7 holes in a 12-hole non-stick muffin tin; don't use paper cases as the mixture will stick to the cases. Stir the vinegar into the milk and leave to stand for a few minutes.

2   Dry toast the pine nuts in a non-stick frying pan over a low heat for 3–4 minutes, stirring frequently until they are light golden brown; take care as they burn easily. Tip the pine nuts onto a plate and leave to cool. Add the oil to the pan and heat for a few seconds, then add the mushrooms and fry over a low heat for 3–4 minutes until lightly cooked. Turn off the heat.

3   Sift the flours, baking powder, bicarbonate of soda and salt into a bowl. Stir in the nutritional yeast, toasted pine nuts and chopped rosemary. Make a hollow in the middle.

4 Pour the milk mixture into the dry ingredients, add the fried mushrooms and melted butter or margarine. Quickly mix everything together until just combined; it should still look very lumpy. Divide evenly among the prepared muffin-tin holes.

5 Put the muffin tin in the oven, then immediately lower the heat to 180°C/fan oven 160°C/gas 4. Bake for 20–25 minutes, or until well risen and golden brown.

6 Place the tin on a wire rack and leave for 5 minutes, then carefully remove the muffins. Serve warm.

BAKER'S TIP

If you don't have any fresh rosemary, use ½ teaspoon dried mixed herbs instead.

Sweet Potato and Herb Muffins

Sweet potatoes and cornmeal give these savoury muffins a lovely golden colour and a slightly sweet flavour which contrasts with the fresh green herbs. Serve them warm if you can.

MAKES 9

225g/8oz oat flour (page 11)
125g/4¼oz fine polenta or fine cornmeal
2 tbsp tapioca flour
2 tsp baking powder
1 tsp bicarbonate of soda
¼ tsp salt
225g/8oz sweet potato puree (see Baker's Tips)
1 tsp lemon juice
5 tbsp plant milk e.g., unsweetened soya or oat milk
2 tbsp chopped fresh parsley
1 tbsp chopped fresh thyme
freshly ground black pepper
1 tbsp sunflower seeds, to sprinkle

1 Preheat the oven to 190°C/fan oven 170°C/gas 5. Grease 9 holes of a 12-hole non-stick muffin tin or line it with 9 paper muffin cases.
2 Put the oat flour, cornmeal, tapioca flour, baking powder, bicarbonate of soda and salt into a bowl and mix to combine. Make a hollow in the middle of the mixture.
3 Mix together the sweet potato puree, lemon juice, plant milk, parsley, thyme and black pepper (to taste) in a jug. Add the wet ingredients to the dry ingredients and stir briefly until just combined.
4 Spoon or ladle the batter into the prepared muffin tin, dividing it evenly among the holes or paper cases. Sprinkle with sunflower seeds. Put the tray in the oven, then

immediately lower the temperature to 180°C/fan oven 160°C/gas 4. Bake for 20–25 minutes, or until well risen and firm to the touch.

5 Leave the muffins in the tins for about 10 minutes before removing and serving warm. Store any uneaten muffins in an airtight tin or container and eat within 2 days of making.

BAKER'S TIPS

The fresh herbs in these muffins give them a lovely fragrant flavour, but if you haven't got fresh, you can substitute with 1 teaspoon dried mixed herbs instead.

To make sweet potato puree, peel 300g/10½oz sweet potatoes, cut into chunks and cook in lightly salted boiling water for 15 minutes, or until tender. Drain in a colander and leave for 5 minutes to let the steam evaporate. Tip back into the pan and mash until very smooth.

Chocolate Chunk Brownies

Black-bean brownies are a well-known and popular vegan bake. Rich, dark and chocolatey, this version is every bit as good as the most decadent high-fat and sugary brownie, but it is much healthier and higher in fibre. The black beans are blended to a thick, floury puree, but no one will notice they are there unless you tell them.

MAKES 9 SQUARES

400g/14oz tin of black beans, drained and rinsed
2 tbsp light muscovado or light brown soft sugar
2 tsp vanilla extract
a pinch of salt
20g/¾oz rolled (porridge) oats
3 tbsp unsweetened cocoa powder
1 tbsp ground flax seeds (linseed)
75g/2¾oz agave syrup
40g/1½oz coconut oil or cocoa butter, melted
½ tsp baking powder
75g/2¾oz vegan dark chocolate, roughly chopped

1   Preheat the oven to 170°C/fan oven 150°C/gas 3. Grease an 18cm (7in) square cake tin and line the base and sides with non-stick baking paper. Put the beans, sugar, vanilla extract and salt into a food processor and blend for a few seconds until the beans are finely chopped. Scrape down the sides with a spatula.
2   Add the oats, cocoa powder, flax seeds, agave syrup and melted coconut oil or cocoa butter, then sprinkle over the baking powder. Blend again for 2–3 minutes until the mixture is fairly smooth.
3   Add the chopped chocolate to the food processor and blend for 10–15 seconds until the chocolate is mixed in but still chunky.

4   Spoon and scrape the mixture into the prepared tin and bake for 20–22 minutes until lightly set (the top should be firm and dry but the centre still slightly soft).
5   Leave the brownies to cool in the tin, then mark into squares. Carefully remove from the tin and cut into squares. Store in an airtight container in the fridge for up to a week.

BAKER'S TIP

These brownies have a slightly fragile texture, so they are best served on plates.

Dark Chocolate and Walnut Brownies

These rich and squidgy brownies are an alternative for those not quite ready to go down the route of brownies made with beans! Try to get golden caster sugar for this recipe, as it has a slight caramel flavour which enhances the brownies.

MAKES 9 SQUARES

2 tbsp ground flax seeds (linseed)
150ml/¼ pint cold strong-brewed coffee
125g/4¼oz vegan dark chocolate, broken into squares
75g/2¾oz plant butter or vegan block margarine
225g/8oz caster sugar, preferably golden unrefined
2 tsp vanilla extract
125g/4¼oz quinoa flour
50g/1¾oz unsweetened cocoa powder
2 tsp baking powder
¼ tsp salt
75g/2¾oz ground almonds
75g/2¾oz walnuts, roughly chopped

1 Preheat the oven to 170°C/fan oven 150°C/gas 3. Grease a 20cm (8in) square cake tin and line the base and sides with non-stick baking paper. Put the ground flax seeds in a small bowl and stir in 6 tablespoons of the coffee. Leave for 5 minutes until the mixture has thickened.

2 Put the squares of chocolate in a heatproof bowl with the rest of the coffee and the butter or margarine. Place the bowl over a pan of very hot water and leave for a few minutes, stirring occasionally, until melted. Remove the bowl from the heat and leave to cool slightly.

3 Stir the sugar and vanilla extract into the chocolate mixture, then sift over the flour, cocoa powder, baking powder and salt.

Add the ground almonds, walnuts and the flax seed mixture. Gently fold everything together until just combined.

4 Spoon and scrape the mixture into the prepared tin, spreading it out into the corners. Bake for 35–40 minutes, or until a fine skewer inserted into the middle of the bake comes out fairly clean with just a few moist crumbs.

5 Put the tin on a wire rack and leave to cool. Carefully remove from the tin, peel off the baking paper and cut into 9 equal squares. Store the brownies in a single layer in an airtight container (keep it in the fridge if the weather is warm) and eat within 5 days.

BAKER'S TIP

Quinoa flour is an excellent addition to rich baked recipes as it is higher in fat than wheat flour and is also high in protein, making it a good choice for vegans.

VARIATION

For chocolate and cherry brownies, leave out the walnuts and stir 75g/2¾oz quartered glacé cherries (preferably natural undyed ones, or glacé morello cherries which have a sweet and sour taste) into the mixture with the ground almonds and flax seed.

Whoopie Pies

The recipe for these delicious little cakes originated with the Amish in New England – they are supposed to get their name from husbands and children exclaiming 'whoopie!' when they opened their lunchboxes and saw the contents. Vegan marshmallows don't melt in the same way as traditional ones, so making a classic marshmallow cream filling is difficult. Instead, here, they are snipped into small pieces and added to a buttercream mixture which is just as delicious.

MAKES 15

3 tbsp aquafaba (page 13)
100g/3½oz caster sugar
50g/1¾oz unsalted plant butter or vegan block margarine, melted
85g/3oz vegan crème fraîche alternative e.g., oat fraîche
1 tbsp plant milk e.g., oat or almond milk
1 tsp vanilla extract
185g/6½oz plain white flour
½ tsp bicarbonate of soda

For the marshmallow cream:
75g/2¾oz vegan marshmallows
50g/1¾oz unsalted plant butter or dairy-free soft margarine, softened
75g/2¾oz icing sugar, sifted, plus extra for dusting
1 tsp vanilla extract

1 Preheat the oven to 180°C/fan oven 160°C/gas 4. Line two baking sheets with non-stick baking paper (if you only have one baking sheet, you'll have to bake in batches).
2 Put the aquafaba into a clean bowl and, using an electric whisk, beat until light and fluffy. Beat in the sugar, a third at a time, until thick and glossy.

3 With the whisk on a low setting, beat in the melted plant butter, vegan crème fraîche alternative, milk and vanilla extract. Sift the flour and bicarbonate of soda over the mixture and beat until just blended.

4 Using a large plain piping nozzle or spoon, pipe or spoon the mixture onto the lined baking sheet in small walnut-sized balls at least 3cm (1¼in) apart, then smooth the tops with the back of a teaspoon dipped in water. Bake for 12–14 minutes until fairly evenly golden on top. Leave to firm up on the baking sheets for a few minutes, then transfer to a wire rack to cool.

5 For the marshmallow cream filling, snip the marshmallows into smaller pieces with clean kitchen scissors. Blend the plant butter and icing sugar together in a bowl, add the vanilla extract, then beat until light and fluffy. Stir in the marshmallows.

6 Spoon and spread the flat side of a whoopie cake with some marshmallow cream, then top with a second whoopie cake (with the marshmallow cream between two flat sides). Dust with a little icing sugar to serve.

VARIATIONS

Chocolate: Melt 75g/2¾oz chopped vegan dark chocolate with the plant butter, use light brown soft sugar instead of caster and replace 25g/1oz of the flour with unsweetened cocoa powder.

Coconut and raspberry: Add 50g/1¾oz desiccated coconut and an extra tablespoon of plant milk (preferably coconut milk) to the cake mixture. Sprinkle the tops with extra desiccated coconut before baking. Beat 2 tablespoons of seedless raspberry jam into the filling.

Lemon: Finely grate the zest from 1 large lemon (preferably unwaxed) and add half to the cake mixture, half to the filling. Decorate the tops with lemon icing: mix 150g/5½oz sifted icing sugar with 1½-2 tbsp freshly squeezed lemon juice.

Cherry and almond: Fold 75g/2¾oz chopped dried sour cherries and 75g/2¾oz finely chopped toasted almonds into the cake mixture and add 2 tablespoons of cherry jam (finely chop the pieces of cherry) into the filling.

Passionfruit: Scoop out the pulp of 3 ripe passionfruit and beat into the filling. Decorate with passionfruit icing: mix 150g/5½oz sifted icing sugar with the pulp of 2 passionfruit. Add a drop or two of cold water if necessary, to get the right consistency.

CHAPTER THREE

Biscuits, Bars and Cookies

....

Ranging from classic favourites such as Chocolate Chip Cookies and Peanut Butter Cookies to dainty Almond Biscotti and elegant French Macarons, you'll find all manner of biscuits in this chapter. Healthy treats, ideal for lunchboxes, are also included, such as Wholemeal Spelt and Walnut Biscuits and Fruit and Nut Clusters. There are also layered slices and bars, which offer a range of tastes and textures in one bake, Millionaire's Shortbread being one of the most familiar. Some of the best recipes in this chapter are so simple that children can help you make them; they'll enjoy helping eat them too.

Chocolate Chip Cookies

Everyone has their own idea of a 'perfect' chocolate chip cookie. Some like a crunchy cookie, others prefer a more chewy texture. This is a combination of the two: crisp edges with a soft squidgy centre. Most will agree that a generous amount of chocolate is a must.

MAKES ABOUT 12

85g/3oz plant butter or vegan block margarine, softened

85g/3oz light muscovado or light brown soft sugar

25g/1oz caster sugar, preferably golden unrefined

1 tsp vanilla extract

200g/7oz plain white flour

1 tsp baking powder

a pinch of salt (optional)

200g/7oz vegan chocolate, chopped, or chocolate chips
(see Baker's Tips)

3 tbsp plant milk e.g., unsweetened soya or oat milk

1 Line two baking sheets with non-stick baking paper. Put the plant butter, sugars and vanilla extract in a bowl and beat together until light and fluffy.

2 Sift over the flour, baking powder and salt (if using). Start to stir in, then add the chocolate and plant milk. Mix to form a soft dough.

3 Shape the dough into 12 equal-sized balls. Flatten each slightly and arrange on the lined baking sheets, spacing them well apart to allow the mixture to spread. Chill the trays in the fridge for 1 hour.

4 About 5 minutes before the end of chilling time, preheat the oven to 200°C/fan oven 180°C/gas 6. Bake the cookies for 10–12 minutes, or until lightly browned around the edges.

5 Place the trays on wire racks and leave for 15 minutes, then carefully remove the cookies and leave to cool on the racks.

These are best served when just cool, before the chocolate sets. When completely cold, store in an airtight tin or container. Eat within 5 days of making.

Peanut Butter Cookies

These protein-packed bakes have a lovely short texture and are delicious as a mid-morning snack or occasional treat. They are rolled in chopped peanuts before baking, which gives them a crunchy coating.

MAKES ABOUT 15

175g/6oz crunchy peanut butter (see Baker's Tips)
50g/1¾oz plant butter or vegan block margarine, softened
50g/1¾oz caster sugar or golden unrefined caster sugar
40g/1½oz light muscovado or light brown soft sugar
1 tsp powdered egg replacer
3 tbsp plant milk, e.g., unsweetened soya or oat milk
125g/4¼oz self-raising white flour
75g/2¾oz unsalted peanuts, roughly chopped

1 Preheat the oven to 180°C/fan oven 160°C/gas 4. Line two baking sheets with non-stick baking paper. Put the peanut butter and plant butter or margarine in a bowl and beat until blended. Add the sugars and beat again until the mixture is lighter in colour and creamy.

2 Blend the egg replacer with 2 teaspoons of the plant milk until smooth, then blend in the rest of the milk. Add to the creamed mixture, then sift over the flour. Mix everything together to make a dough.

3 Put the chopped peanuts on a plate. Shape the cookie mixture into about 15 balls, slightly bigger than a walnut, then roll in the chopped peanuts to coat them all over.

4 Put the cookies on the lined baking sheets, spacing them well apart to allow the mixture to spread, then flatten each ball slightly (this will stop them rolling off the baking sheets).

5 Bake for 10–12 minutes until firm, then remove them from the oven. Allow the cookies to cool on the baking sheets for 3–4

minutes, then transfer to a wire rack and leave to cool completely. Store in an airtight tin or container for up to a week.

Wholemeal Spelt and Walnut Biscuits

Spelt is an ancient grain related to wheat and it has a lovely nutty texture. It still contains a small amount of gluten, so while it is unsuitable for those with coeliac disease, some who have a slight intolerance to wheat can tolerate spelt. The grains can be milled to make either white flour or wholemeal, as used here.

MAKES 20

125g/4¼oz wholemeal spelt flour
1 tsp ground cinnamon
½ tsp baking powder
a pinch of salt
3 tbsp walnut oil or sunflower oil
75g/2¾oz maple syrup or carob and maple syrup blend
20 walnut halves
1 tsp icing sugar, preferably golden unrefined icing sugar

1 Preheat the oven to 190°C/fan oven 170°C/gas 5. Line a large baking sheet with non-stick baking paper. Sift the flour, ¾ teaspoon of the cinnamon, the baking powder and salt into a bowl and stir together to mix.

2 Put the oil in a small jug and add the maple syrup, then stir together. Drizzle over the dry ingredients and mix to form a soft dough.

3 Divide the dough into 20 pieces and roll each into a ball. Arrange on the lined baking sheet, spacing them slightly apart to allow room for them to spread. Top each ball of dough with a walnut half, pressing down lightly while doing this to flatten the balls very slightly.

4 Bake for 10–12 minutes until slightly darker in colour. Leave to cool on the baking sheet for 2–3 minutes, then transfer to a wire rack.

5 Mix the icing sugar and remaining ¼ teaspoon of cinnamon together in a small bowl and lightly dust the tops of the biscuits while they are still warm. Leave to cool completely. Store the biscuits in an airtight tin or container for up to 10 days.

VARIATION

Instead of whole nuts, scatter the tops with 25g/1oz chopped walnuts, pressing them down lightly. Make a filling by creaming together 50g/1¾oz softened plant butter or vegan block margarine, 100g/3½oz sifted icing sugar, preferably golden unrefined, and 1 tablespoon maple syrup (or carob and maple syrup blend) and use to sandwich the biscuits together in pairs.

Fruit and Nut Clusters

If you are looking for a healthier cookie, these are a good choice. The fruit is moistened with fruit juice to make it sticky, before combining with the rest of the ingredients, so that the mixture holds together without needing eggs to bind it.

MAKES 15

50g/1¾oz dried dates, finely chopped
50g/1¾oz ready-to-eat dried apricots, finely chopped
4 tbsp apple or orange juice
2 tbsp walnut, rapeseed or sunflower oil
50g/1¾oz barley flakes
50g/1¾oz unsalted mixed nuts e.g., Brazil nuts, walnuts and
    hazelnuts, finely chopped
50g/1¾oz sunflower seeds, chopped
50g/1¾oz self-raising wholemeal flour
½ tsp baking powder
a pinch of salt (optional)

1 Put the dates and apricots in a mixing bowl and sprinkle over the fruit juice. Leave to soak for a few minutes while preparing the rest of the ingredients.
2 Preheat the oven to 190°C/fan oven 170°C/gas 5. Lightly grease a large baking sheet or line with non-stick baking paper.
3 Drizzle the oil over the fruit and stir, then stir in the barley flakes. Add all the remaining ingredients and stir until everything sticks together.
4 Scoop out heaped teaspoonfuls of the mixture, then using slightly dampened hands, roll each spoonful into a ball to make 15 balls. Press into rounds about 5cm (2in) in diameter and arrange on the lined baking sheet, spacing them slightly apart to allow them to spread a little.

5 Bake for 10–12 minutes, or until lightly browned on top. Leave on the baking sheet for 2–3 minutes to firm up, then carefully transfer to a wire rack and leave to cool. When cold, store in an airtight tin or container; they will keep for up to 5 days.

BAKER'S TIP

Barley flakes have a subtle nutty taste and work well in these cookies, but if you don't have any, you can use rolled (porridge) oats here instead.

Ice-box Cookies

The predecessor to the fridge, ice-boxes were simply chests with a compartment for a large block of ice and another for food. This type of cookie originated in America in the 19th century – ice-box cookies are made from a soft dough which must be well-chilled before slicing and baking.

MAKES ABOUT 16

200g/7oz unsalted plant butter, softened
100g/3½oz icing sugar, plus extra for dusting
1 tsp vanilla extract
75g/2¾oz rolled (porridge) oats
200g/7oz plain white flour
25g/1oz chickpea flour, besan (gram) flour or extra plain
    white flour
½ tsp baking powder

1   Put the butter in a mixing bowl. Sift over the icing sugar, then beat with a wooden spoon or an electric whisk on low speed until the mixture is light and creamy. Beat in the vanilla extract, then stir in the oats.

2   Sift the flours and baking powder over the creamed mixture. Stir together, then use your hands to make a soft dough. Shape into a log 7–8cm (2¾–3in) in diameter, then wrap in non-stick baking paper or cling film and chill in the fridge for at least 30 minutes, or until firm.

3   Preheat the oven to 160°C/fan 140°C/gas 3. Line a baking sheet with non-stick baking paper. Slice the log into rounds about 5mm (¼in) thick – about 16 rounds in total – and place on the lined baking sheet, spacing them slightly apart to allow room for them to spread.

4   Bake for 14–18 minutes, or until golden brown around the edges. Remove from the oven and lightly dust with icing sugar.

Leave on the tray for 2–3 minutes, then carefully remove and cool on a wire rack. Store in an airtight tin or container and eat within 5 days of making.

BAKER'S TIP

The roll of dough can be kept in the fridge for a week or two or can be frozen if preferred; it will keep for up to 3–4 months. Remove from the freezer and thaw in the fridge for several hours before slicing and baking.

Ginger Oatmeal Cookies

Oats are great in vegan baking because they help to bind the mixture and together with aquafaba make a firm, not too crumbly cookie. These are great for packed lunches and picnics as they will retain their shape.

MAKES 14

4 tbsp aquafaba (page 13)
a pinch of salt (optional)
25g/1oz rolled (porridge) oats
25g/1oz oat flour (page 11)
50g/1¾oz ground almonds
50g/1¾oz coconut oil, melted
2 balls of stem ginger in syrup, finely chopped
2 tbsp stem ginger syrup from the jar

1 Preheat the oven to 180°C/fan oven 160°C/gas 4. Line a large baking sheet with non-stick baking paper.
2 Put the aquafaba in a bowl and whisk with a hand-held whisk or a fork until frothy. Stir in the remaining ingredients until thoroughly mixed.
3 Scoop out heaped teaspoons of the mixture and drop onto the lined baking sheet. Press them out into rounds about 1cm (½in) thick. Make the rest of the cookies in the same way – you should have 14 in total.
4 Bake for about 20 minutes, or until the cookies are golden brown. Leave on the baking sheet for 3–4 minutes to firm up a little, then transfer to a wire rack to cool (or serve them slightly warm if you prefer). Store in an airtight tin or container and eat within 5 days of making.

BAKER'S TIPS

If you love very gingery cookies, add ½ teaspoon of ground ginger to the mixture as well as the stem ginger.

These cookies can be made gluten-free providing you choose gluten-free oats.

Tahini Cookies

Instead of buying protein bars and balls for eating before or after a workout – or just as an in-between meal snack – make these cookies: a couple of them will provide the boost you need. Tahini has a massive 25g/1oz of protein per 100g/3½oz and provides a number of useful minerals, including calcium which can be short supply when you don't eat dairy foods.

MAKES ABOUT 14

60g/2¼oz coconut oil, at room temperature
60g/2¼oz tahini
40g/1½oz caster sugar
25g/1oz light muscovado or light brown soft sugar
1 tbsp plant milk e.g., unsweetened soya or oat milk
½ tsp vanilla extract
80g/2¾oz plain white flour
1 tbsp cornflour
¼ tsp baking powder
¼ tsp bicarbonate of soda
a pinch of salt (optional)
2 tbsp sesame seeds

1   Put the coconut oil, tahini and sugars in a bowl and mix together until soft and creamy. Stir in the plant milk and vanilla extract.
2   Sift over the flour, cornflour, baking powder, bicarbonate of soda and salt (if using) and stir everything together. Put the bowl in the fridge and chill for 20 minutes.
3   Preheat the oven to 170°C/fan oven 150°C/gas 3. Line two baking sheets with non-stick baking paper. Shape heaped teaspoonfuls of the dough into balls, slightly bigger than the size of a walnut – you should have about 14 balls. Roll in the sesame seeds to coat, then arrange on the lined baking sheet,

pressing down a little to flatten slightly and stop them rolling off the sheet. Space them well apart to allow room for them to spread.

4   Bake for about 12 minutes, or until lightly browned around the edges. Leave on the baking sheet for 15 minutes, then remove and transfer to a wire rack to cool completely. Store the cookies in an airtight tin or container. They will keep for up to 5 days.

BAKER'S TIP

Tahini, a creamy paste simply made by grinding sesame seeds, tends to separate in the jar, with the sesame seed oil floating to the top. Give it a good stir to mix the paste and oil together before using. Choose a light coloured, mild-flavoured version for this recipe, made from ground hulled seeds.

VARIATIONS

For chocolate tahini cookies, substitute 25g/1oz unsweetened cocoa powder for 25g/1oz of the flour.

For chocolate chip tahini cookies, stir 75g/2¾oz vegan chocolate chips or roughly chopped vegan chocolate into the dry ingredients in step 2.

Orange and Walnut Shortbreads

Walnuts are a great source of omega-3 for vegans and add a delicious flavour to these shortbread biscuits. They are made with sunflower margarine using the creaming method rather than rubbing the fat into the flour as in traditional shortbread. It gives them a lighter, crisper texture.

MAKES ABOUT 15

125g/4¼oz sunflower margarine
50g/1¾oz caster sugar, preferably golden unrefined, plus extra for sprinkling
finely grated zest of 1 orange, preferably unwaxed
50g/1¾oz plain white flour, plus extra for dusting
50g/1¾oz plain wholemeal flour
50g/1¾oz brown rice flour
50g/1¾oz walnuts, finely chopped
a pinch of salt (optional)

1 Put the margarine, sugar and orange zest in a bowl and cream together until light and fluffy. Sift over the flours, adding the bran left in the sieve, then add the walnuts and salt (if using). Mix together to make a soft dough.
2 Turn out onto a lightly floured work surface and knead for just a few seconds until smooth. Shape the dough into a cylinder about 15cm (6in) long. Wrap in cling film (or plastic-free alternative) and chill in the fridge for 1 hour.
3 Towards the end of chilling time, preheat the oven to 190°C/fan oven 170°C/gas 5. Line a baking sheet with non-stick baking paper.
4 Unwrap the biscuit dough and cut it into about 15 slices with a sharp knife. Turn the cylinder of dough a little after each cut, so that it keeps its round shape. Place the biscuits on the lined baking sheet, spacing them apart a little to allow room for them to spread.

5 Bake for 12–15 minutes until dark golden. After baking, sprinkle the tops with a little extra caster sugar. Leave on the baking sheet for 5 minutes, then remove and cool on a wire rack. Store in an airtight container or tin. The shortbreads will keep for up to a week.

BAKER'S TIPS

For sugar-crusted cookies, roll the edge of the dough in granulated or demerara sugar before slicing and baking instead of dusting with sugar after baking.

For a more 'buttery' shortbread, use finely chopped macadamia nuts instead of walnuts; they give the biscuits a wonderful rich flavour.

Classic Millionaire's Shortbread

This rich and super-sweet well-known treat has a 'buttery' shortbread base, thick caramel filling and a chocolate topping. Sweetened condensed coconut milk makes a great vegan substitute for sweetened condensed dairy milk – it has a slight coconut flavour which works well here.

MAKES 9 LARGE OR 16 SMALL SQUARES

For the shortbread base:
250g/9oz plain white flour
75g/2¾oz caster sugar
175g/6oz cold plant butter or vegan block margarine

For the caramel layer:
150g/5½oz plant butter or vegan block margarine
150g/5½oz light muscovado or light brown soft sugar
3½ tbsp golden syrup
320–370g (11½–13oz) tin of vegan condensed milk or
  sweetened condensed coconut milk
a pinch of salt

For the chocolate topping:
200g/7oz vegan dark or milk chocolate, roughly chopped
1 tsp rapeseed oil or sunflower oil

1 Preheat the oven to 180°C/fan oven 160°C/gas 4. Lightly grease a 20cm (8in) square cake tin and line the base with non-stick baking paper.
2 For the shortbread base, sift the flour into a bowl, then stir in the sugar. Cut the butter or margarine into small cubes, add to the flour and sugar and rub in with your fingertips until the mixture resembles fine breadcrumbs. Lightly squeeze the mixture together until it forms a dough, then press into the base of the tin in an even layer.

3 Prick the shortbread all over with a fork and bake for 18–20 minutes, or until firm to the touch and very lightly browned. Remove from the oven and leave (still in the tin) to cool on a wire rack.

4 To make the caramel layer, put the plant butter and sugar in a large, wide heavy-based saucepan and gently heat, stirring until the sugar has dissolved. Add the syrup, condensed milk and salt. Turn up the heat and simmer, stirring frequently, for 10–15 minutes, or until the mixture has thickened slightly. Remove from the heat, leave until it stops bubbling, then pour it over the shortbread and leave to cool and set (this can take up to 1 hour).

5 For the chocolate topping, put the chocolate and oil into a heatproof bowl and place over a pan of very hot water. Leave for a few minutes, until melted, stirring occasionally. Remove from the heat, leave for 3–4 minutes, then pour and spread over the caramel topping. Leave to cool and set.

6 Mark into squares, then chill in the fridge for 30 minutes. Cut into squares with a hot knife (dip into hot water, then wipe dry on a piece of kitchen paper), then carefully remove from the tin. Store in a single layer in an airtight tin or container and eat within 5 days. In warmer weather, keep in the fridge.

BAKER'S TIP

The shortbread base should be a little browner than a traditional dairy-butter shortbread to achieve the same texture and crispness.

Coconut Macaroons

Usually made with whisked egg whites, these moist and tender macaroons are a cross between a cake and a cookie. Soft and chewy on the inside, crisp and golden on the outside, don't confuse these with macarons – they are two very different bakes.

MAKES 10

75g/2¾oz unsweetened desiccated coconut
100g/3½oz ground almonds
25g/1oz flaked almonds
1/2 tsp baking powder
a pinch of bicarbonate of soda
a pinch of salt
6 tbsp maple syrup or maple and carob syrup blend
60g/2¼oz apple puree (page 12)
60g/2¼oz coconut oil, melted

1 Preheat the oven to 180°C/fan oven 160°C/gas 4. Line a baking sheet with non-stick baking paper. Put the coconut, ground and flaked almonds, baking powder, bicarbonate of soda and salt in a bowl and stir together until well mixed.

2 Put the maple syrup, apple puree and melted coconut oil in a bowl and stir together. Add the dry ingredients and mix together.

3 Scoop up spoonfuls of the mixture and using damp hands, roll into 10 balls. Arrange them on the lined baking sheet, spacing them apart to allow them room to spread, and gently press down a little to stop them rolling off the sheet.

4 Bake for 14–15 minutes, or until the macaroons are lightly browned. Allow them to cool for 5 minutes on the baking sheet, then remove and cool on a wire rack. Store in an airtight tin or container and eat within 5 days of making.

BAKER'S TIP

If you want to dip the macaroons in chocolate, break 100g/3½oz vegan dark chocolate into squares and place in a heatproof bowl. Melt in the microwave, stopping to stir every 20 seconds, until almost melted (the chocolate will carry on melting in the residual heat). Alternatively, place the bowl over a pan of very hot water, stirring after a few minutes until smooth. Dip the bases of the macaroons in the chocolate and return to the lined baking sheet chocolate side down to set.

VARIATION

For chocolate hazelnut macaroons, use 75g/2¾oz apple puree and substitute ground hazelnuts and chopped skinned hazelnuts for the ground and flaked almonds and add 1 tablespoon of unsweetened cocoa powder to the dry ingredients.

French Macarons

These dainty and delicate almond cookies have crisp outsides and a moist, slightly chewy centre. They are sandwiched together in pairs. They do take time and care to make but are worth the effort.

MAKES ABOUT 20

100g/3½oz icing sugar
150g/5½oz almond flour or very fine ground almonds
100ml/3½fl oz aquafaba (page 13)
¼ tsp cream of tartar
125g/4¼oz granulated sugar

For the filling:
50g/1¾oz plant butter, softened
150g/5½oz icing sugar, sifted
1 tsp vanilla extract
a drop of vegan food colouring paste (optional)

1 Line two baking sheets with non-stick baking paper and draw 4cm (1½in) circles on the paper, leaving a small amount of space between the circles to allow the macarons to spread slightly. Flip the paper, so that the pencil lines are underneath (make sure you draw them so that they can be seen through the paper).
2 Sift the icing sugar into a bowl and stir in the almond flour. Put the aquafaba and cream of tartar in another bowl and using a hand-held electric whisk, whisk at low speed for a minute or two, then turn up to maximum speed and beat until the mixture holds stiff peaks; this will take 4–5 minutes. Gradually whisk in the granulated sugar, a spoonful at a time, until the mixture forms thick, glossy peaks when the whisk is lifted; this can take a further 4–5 minutes.
3 Add the icing sugar and almond flour mixture to the aquafaba and fold in with a spatula, knocking out most of the air. Keep

folding until the mixture forms a thick ribbon that slowly blends back into itself.

4   Spoon half of the mixture into a piping bag fitted with a 1cm (½in) plain nozzle. Hold the bag vertically and pipe the mixture to fit just inside the drawn circles. Repeat with the remaining mixture. Bang the trays down hard on the work surface a few times to burst any air bubbles, then leave the trays at room temperature for about 1½ hours, or until the macarons have formed a dry 'skin'.

5   Five to ten minutes before baking, preheat the oven to 140°C/fan oven 120°C/gas 1. Bake the macarons for 10 minutes, then rotate the baking sheets and bake for a further 10 minutes. Remove from the oven and allow them to cool completely on the sheets.

6   For the filling, beat the plant butter in a bowl until soft. Gradually beat in the icing sugar, then add the vanilla extract and a drop or two of colouring paste (if using). Continue to beat until light. Use to sandwich the macarons together in pairs. Store in an airtight container or tin and eat within 2 days.

BAKER'S TIP

Almond flour is simply very fine ground almonds and some brands are a lot finer than others, so do check before buying. Ideally the almond flour or ground almonds should be a pure creamy white colour without any flecks of almond skins in them, so buy in clear packets so you can see the product.

Almond Biscotti

These are perfect with after-dinner coffee or liqueurs such as Amaretto or Limoncello, or to serve with desserts such as ice cream or granita.

MAKES 10

125g/4¼oz plain white flour, plus extra for dusting
¼ tsp bicarbonate of soda
¼ tsp baking powder
a pinch of salt
60g/2¼oz ground almonds
50g/1¾oz blanched hazelnuts, finely chopped
50g/1¾oz caster sugar
40g/1½oz apple puree (page 12)
3 tbsp light olive oil
3 tbsp Amaretto liqueur

1 Preheat the oven to 180°C/fan oven 160°C/gas 4. Line a large baking sheet with non-stick baking parchment. Sift the flour, bicarbonate of soda, baking powder and salt into a bowl. Stir in the ground almonds and chopped hazelnuts.

2 Mix the sugar, apple puree, olive oil and Amaretto together in a jug. Add to the dry ingredients and gently mix together to make a soft dough.

3 Turn out the dough on a lightly floured surface and shape into a log about 4cm (1½in) in diameter. Flatten slightly, then transfer to the baking sheet and bake for 30 minutes until lightly browned on top.

4 Remove from the oven and leave it to cool for a few minutes. Turn down the oven temperature to 160°C/fan 140°C/gas 3.

5 Cut the log into 10 slices and put them back on the baking sheet. Bake for a further 10 minutes, then turn the biscuits and cook for a final 5–6 minutes until crisp. Transfer to a wire

rack and leave them to cool. Store in an airtight container or
tin; they will keep for up to a week.

BAKER'S TIP

You can use any type of nuts for these, but make sure you keep to
the same weights of ground and chopped nuts.

Blueberry and Banana Breakfast Bars

These are perfect for those who don't feel like eating breakfast first thing and just want to take something to eat with them when they leave the house. They are equally good as a mid-morning or mid-afternoon snack.

MAKES 16 BARS

150g/5½oz plant butter or vegan block margarine
125g/4¼oz light muscovado or light brown soft sugar
4 tbsp maple syrup
2 tsp vanilla extract
300g/10½oz rolled (porridge) oats
75g/2¾oz flaked almonds
25g/1oz sesame seeds
3 small ripe bananas
75g/2¾oz almond butter or peanut butter (page 12)
150g/5½oz fresh blueberries

1 Preheat the oven to 170°C/fan oven 150°C/gas 3. Lightly grease a 25cm (10in) square cake tin and line the base with non-stick baking paper.
2 Cut the butter into pieces and put in a heavy-based saucepan. Add the sugar and maple syrup and gently heat, stirring frequently, until the butter has melted. Remove from the heat and stir in the vanilla extract.
3 Put the oats, almonds and sesame seeds in a mixing bowl and stir together. Peel the bananas and mash until fairly smooth, then mix with the almond or peanut butter. Add to the bowl with the melted mixture and the blueberries. Stir everything together until combined.
4 Tip into the prepared tin, level the top, then bake for 25–30 minutes, or until golden. Allow to cool in the tin, then turn out onto a board, remove the baking paper and cut into 16 bars.

BAKER'S TIP

You can use frozen blueberries for making these bars but defrost them first on kitchen paper or they may make the bake too wet.

Cherry and Almond Slices

These are a cross between a flapjack and a cake and contain both dried cherries and sticky cherry jam for maximum flavour and a variety of textures. They can easily be made gluten-free by using gluten-free flour and oats.

MAKES 14

200g/7oz rolled (porridge) oats
50g/1¾oz plain wholewheat flour
50g/1¾oz ground almonds
175g/6oz dairy-free vegan margarine
2 tbsp maple syrup
25g/1oz dried cherries, chopped
1 tsp almond extract (optional)
4 tbsp cherry jam

1 Preheat the oven to 180°C/fan oven 160°C/gas 4. Lightly grease a 23cm (9in) square cake tin and line the base with non-stick baking paper.
2 Put the oats, flour and ground almonds in a bowl and stir to mix. Put the margarine, maple syrup and dried cherries in a saucepan. Heat gently, stirring occasionally, until the margarine has melted. Stir in the almond extract (if using).
3 Add the melted mixture to the dry ingredients and mix well. Spoon half the mixture into the tin, pressing it down firmly with the back of the spoon. Spread the jam over the top, almost but not quite to the edge, leaving a 3–4mm gap (this will prevent the jam sticking to the tin, which would make the slices harder to remove). Alternatively, completely line the tin (base and sides) with non-stick baking paper.
4 Spoon over the rest of the oat mixture, levelling and firming the top with the back of the spoon or your fingers. Bake for 25–30 minutes, or until the top is a dark golden brown.

5 Remove from the oven and leave the tin to cool on a wire rack before marking into 14 slices, or squares if you prefer. Chill in the fridge for 20 minutes, then remove from the tin and cut into the pieces you have marked. Keep in an airtight container in the fridge. Eat within a week of making.

VARIATION

For apricot and almond slices, use 50g/1¾oz dried apricots snipped into tiny pieces instead of the dried cherries and apricot jam instead of cherry jam.

CHAPTER FOUR

Sweet and Savoury Pastries

....

Few can resist the crumbly texture of a rich fruit tart or a warm savoury starter or snack encased in crisp light pastry. From elegant sweet pies and continental pastries with delectable fillings to savoury quiche, samosas and pasties, the recipes in this chapter are people pleasers. Vegans can still enjoy a slice of quiche or a 'sausage' roll – meat-free of course – and a platter of hot mince pies without worrying about the ingredients used in either the pastry or filling.

For those who avoid dairy, cheesecakes may seem off-limits, but they don't have to be and finally you can enjoy a slice of lemon meringue pie with a tangy lemon curd filling and light-as-air meringue topping made without eggs or butter; once you know how, it's easy.

Vegan 'Sausage' Rolls

Don't let meat-eaters tell you that the word 'sausage' can only be used for meat products; the word has been used for plant-based recipes as well for more than two hundred years. Chopped nuts and borlotti beans ensure these vegan sausage rolls contain a good amount of protein as well as texture.

If time allows, make the filling ahead and chill in the fridge to firm it so that it is easier to shape.

MAKES 12

1 large sweet potato, weighing about 175g/6oz
320–375g/11½–13oz packet ready-rolled vegan puff pastry
1 tbsp rapeseed oil or sunflower oil
1 small red onion, peeled and finely chopped
1 garlic clove, peeled and crushed (optional)
2 tsp smoked paprika
2 tbsp sun-dried tomato puree
400g/14oz tin of borlotti beans, rinsed and drained
50g/1¾oz Brazil nuts, chopped
4 tbsp chopped fresh parsley
salt and freshly ground black pepper
1–2 tbsp plant milk e.g., unsweetened soya or oat milk, for brushing
2 tbsp sesame seeds

1   Prick the sweet potato several times with a fork and microwave on high for 6–7 minutes, or until tender. Remove and leave until cool enough to handle, then peel off the skin. Remove the puff pastry from the fridge and leave at room temperature.

2   Heat the oil in a frying pan over a medium heat, add the onion and cook for 5–6 minutes, stirring frequently. Add the garlic (if using) and cook for a further minute, or until the onion is

just soft but not beginning to colour. Turn off the heat, then stir in the smoked paprika and tomato puree.

3 Put the warm sweet potato into a bowl and mash until smooth. Add the beans and continue mashing to roughly break up the beans. Stir in the onion mixture, nuts and parsley and season with salt and pepper. Leave to cool.

4 Preheat the oven to 220°C/fan oven 200°C/gas 7. Line a baking sheet with non-stick baking paper, unroll the sheet of puff pastry and cut it into two long rectangles. Form half of the sweet potato filling into a sausage shape along the middle of one of the rectangles. Brush the borders with milk, then fold one edge of the pastry over the filling and use a fork to firmly press the edges together.

5 Repeat with the second piece of pastry and remaining filling, then cut each long pastry roll into 6 'sausage' rolls with a sharp knife. Alternatively, cut each long pastry roll into 8 to make 16 snack-sized sausage rolls. Brush the tops with milk and sprinkle with the sesame seeds. Place on the lined baking sheet.

6 Bake for 20 minutes, or until the pastry is cooked and a deep golden brown. Leave to cool on the sheet for 5 minutes, then remove and serve hot or allow to cool on a wire rack. When cold, store in an airtight container in the fridge and eat within 3 days of making.

Creamy Spinach Quiche

Instead of a traditional egg-based filling, the crisp pastry case of this quiche contains a spinach mixture baked in a lightly set savoury custard made with tofu and vegan cream.

SERVES 6

For the pastry:
2 tsp ground flax seeds (linseed)
2 tbsp water
150g/5½oz plain white flour, plus extra for dusting
a pinch of salt
a pinch of ground turmeric (optional)
65g/2½oz cold plant butter

For the filling:
1 tbsp olive oil
6 spring onions, trimmed and thinly sliced
250g/9oz fresh baby spinach leaves
350g/12oz silken tofu
1 tbsp chickpea flour, besan (gram) flour or cornflour
¼ tsp ground turmeric (optional)
6 tbsp vegan cream e.g., oat or soya cream
1 tbsp nutritional yeast
freshly ground black pepper
25g/1oz finely grated vegan parmesan or vegan mature Cheddar

1   To make the pastry, put the ground flax seeds (linseed) in a small bowl with the water and whisk together with a fork. Leave for a few minutes to thicken. Sift the flour, salt and turmeric (if using) into a bowl. Cut the plant butter into small cubes, add to the flour and rub in with your fingertips until the mixture resembles fine breadcrumbs. Add the flax seed mixture and stir together to make a firm dough. Knead gently on a lightly floured surface for a few seconds until smooth. Shape into a ball and flatten into a round disc, then flatten slightly (this makes it easier when it comes to rolling out). Wrap in cling film (or plastic-free alternative) and chill in the fridge for 20 minutes.

2   Roll out the pastry on a lightly floured surface and use to line a 22–23cm (8½–9in) loose-bottomed flan tin. Chill for a further 20 minutes. Towards the end of the chilling time, put a baking sheet in the oven and preheat to 200°C/fan oven 180°C/gas 6.

3   Prick the base of the pastry case with a fork and line with non-stick baking paper or foil, pressing it neatly into the corners. Weigh the paper down with dried beans or ceramic baking beans. Bake in the oven on the heated baking sheet for 15 minutes, then remove the paper or foil and beans and bake for a further 5 minutes.

4   While the pastry is chilling and baking, make the filling. Heat the oil in a wok or large saucepan over a medium-low heat, add the spring onions and fry gently for 3–4 minutes. Add the spinach, cover with a lid and steam for 4 minutes, or until wilted and tender. Drain in a colander, squeezing out as much liquid as possible.

5   Drain any liquid from the tofu and put it in a food processor. Blend the chickpea flour and turmeric (if using) with 1 tablespoon of the vegan cream. Stir in the remaining cream, then add to the tofu with the nutritional yeast. Season with freshly ground black pepper, then blend to a smooth puree. Tip into a bowl, then stir in the drained spinach and spring onions.

6   Spoon the spinach and tofu mixture into the pastry case, levelling the top smooth with the back of the spoon. Scatter over the grated cheese.

7   Return the tart to the oven, then turn down the temperature to 180°C/fan oven 160°C/gas 4. Bake for 25 minutes, or until the top is golden brown and the filling is just set. Leave to cool in the tin for 10 minutes, then remove the tart and serve warm.

BAKER'S TIP

If you prefer, make the quiche with almond-butter pastry (page 148).

Cheese and Onion Pasties

Puff pastry is time-consuming to make but fortunately most brands of ready-made are vegan – just check the label as a few are 'butter-enriched' so not suitable. Even better, you can buy ready-rolled sheets of pastry which makes these light and crispy pasties a doddle.

MAKES 6

320–375g/11½–13oz packet ready-rolled vegan puff pastry
1 tbsp rapeseed oil or sunflower oil
6 spring onions, trimmed and thinly sliced
150g/5½oz floury potatoes, such as King Edward, peeled and cut into 5mm (¼in) dice
1 tbsp wholegrain mustard
salt and freshly ground black pepper
plain flour, for dusting
100g/3½oz vegan Cheddar, grated
2 tbsp plant milk e.g., unsweetened soya or oat milk, for glazing
a tiny pinch of ground turmeric (optional)

1   Remove the pastry from the fridge and leave it, still wrapped, at room temperature for 15 minutes. Line a baking sheet with non-stick baking paper.
2   Heat the oil in a frying pan over a medium-low heat, add the spring onions and potatoes and cook gently for 5 minutes, stirring frequently until the onions are just soft and the potatoes are starting to soften. Add 1 tablespoon of water to the pan if the mixture starts to stick. Set aside to cool a little, then stir in the mustard and season with salt and freshly ground black pepper. Leave to cool.
3   Preheat the oven to 220°C/fan oven 200°C/gas 7. Unroll the sheet of puff pastry on a lightly floured work surface and cut into six even rectangles; these will measure about 11 x 12cm

$(4\frac{1}{2}-4\frac{3}{4}$in) depending on the brand of pastry. Brush a little milk around the edges of each.

4   Stir the grated cheese into the potato mixture, then divide the filling evenly among the pastry rectangles, spooning it to the right of the middle and leaving a 1cm ($\frac{1}{2}$in) gap around the edges. Fold the other side of the pastry rectangle over the filling to make a sausage roll-shaped pasty, then press the edges together with floured fingers to seal and crimp with a fork.

5   Transfer the pasties to the lined baking sheet and brush the tops with plant milk mixed with a pinch of ground turmeric if liked, to give it a golden colour. Make a small slit in the top of each pastry to allow steam to escape. Put in the oven then lower the temperature to 200°C/fan oven 180°C/gas 6. Bake for about 20 minutes, or until well risen, dark golden and crisp. Allow to cool on the baking sheet for 5 minutes before serving hot or transfer to a wire rack and leave to cool.

BAKER'S TIP

Leaving the pastry at room temperature for a few minutes before unrolling it will help prevent it cracking when you make the pasties.

Spicy Samosas

Filo pastry is naturally vegan (although you should always check the packet first). These spicy pastry triangles are baked rather than deep-fried, which reduces their fat content. They contain almonds and peas which are both good sources of protein for vegans. Delicious served hot or cold with a fresh mango chutney, or add a mixed salad for a perfect light lunch.

MAKES 12

2 sheets of filo pastry measuring about 30 x 50cm (12 x 20in)
   (weighing about 65g/2½oz in total)
2 tbsp rapeseed oil or sunflower oil

For the filling:
1 potato, about 150g/5½oz, peeled and cut into 6–7mm
   (about ¼in) dice
1 small carrot, peeled and diced
50g/1¾oz frozen peas
1 tbsp curry paste
50g/1¾oz flaked almonds
2 tbsp chopped fresh coriander
salt and freshly ground black pepper
1 tbsp sesame seeds

For the mango salsa:
1 tsp rapeseed oil or sunflower oil
1 tsp lemon juice
a pinch of caster sugar
a pinch of crushed dried red chillies
1 tsp freshly grated root ginger
1 ripe mango, cut into small dice
1 tsp freshly grated root ginger

1 Remove the pastry from the fridge and leave it, still wrapped, at room temperature while preparing the filling. Cook the diced potato and carrot in a saucepan of lightly salted boiling water for 6 minutes. Add the peas, keep on the heat for a further 30 seconds to allow them to defrost, then drain well.

2 Tip the vegetables into a bowl and gently stir in the curry paste and a little black pepper, making sure you don't break up the vegetables too much. Leave to cool then stir in the almonds and coriander.

3 Preheat the oven to 200°C/fan oven 180°C/gas 6. Line a baking sheet with non-stick baking paper. Take one sheet of the filo (keep the other covered to stop it drying out). Cut lengthways into 6 strips, each about 30cm (12in) long. Lightly brush all over with the oil.

4 Put a rounded tablespoonful of the filling in the middle of one end of the pastry. Take one corner and fold it diagonally over the filling to make a triangle, flattening the filling a little, then continue folding the strip over in a triangular shape until you come to the end. Put the pastry seam-side down on the prepared baking sheet.

5 Repeat with the remaining pastry and filling to make 12 samosas. Brush with the remaining oil and sprinkle with the sesame seeds. Bake for 12–15 minutes, or until golden brown.

6 To make the mango salsa, combine all the ingredients together in a bowl. Serve the samosas hot or cold with the salsa, or with vegan yogurt or chutney .

Pumpkin Pie

This creamy, delicately spiced pumpkin pie is a classic American Thanksgiving dessert, usually made with an egg-set custard. Here it is made with silken tofu which allows the flavour of the pumpkin to dominate. An almond-butter pastry complements the filling.

SERVES 8

For the almond-butter pastry:
100g/3½oz plant butter or vegan block margarine, softened
1½ tbsp smooth almond butter
175g/6oz plain white flour, plus extra for dusting
2 tbsp cold water

For the filling:
400g/14oz pumpkin or butternut squash, peeled, deseeded and cut into chunks
150g/5½oz silken tofu
1 tsp ground cinnamon
½ tsp ground allspice or mixed spice
¼ tsp freshly grated nutmeg
100g/3½oz light muscovado, light brown soft sugar or coconut sugar
6 tbsp maple syrup or carob and maple syrup blend
2 tsp cornflour
a pinch of salt (optional)

non-dairy cream or vegan ice cream, to serve

1   For the pastry, blend the plant butter with the almond butter in a bowl until mixed. Scoop out onto a piece of baking paper and chill in the freezer for 10 minutes. Sift the flour into the bowl, then add the butter and nut butter blend, cut into small pieces, and rub in until the mixture resembles fine breadcrumbs. Stir in enough of the cold water to make a dough.

2   Lightly knead for just a few seconds on a floured surface until smooth to make a ball, then flatten slightly (this makes it easier when it comes to rolling out), wrap in cling film (or plastic-free alternative) and chill in the fridge for 15 minutes. Put a baking sheet in the oven and preheat the oven to 190°C/fan oven 170°C/gas 5.

3   While the pastry is chilling, put the pumpkin chunks into a saucepan and pour over just enough water to cover. Bring to the boil, cover with a lid and simmer for 15 minutes, or until tender. Drain well and set aside.

4   Roll out the pastry and use to line a 23cm (9in) loose-bottomed fluted flan tin. Prick the base of the pastry case with a fork and line with non-stick baking paper or foil, pressing it neatly into the corners. Weigh the paper down with dried beans or ceramic baking beans. Put the flan case in the oven on the heated baking sheet. Turn down the temperature to 180°C/fan oven 160°C/gas 4 and bake for 10 minutes, then remove the paper or foil and beans and bake for a further 5 minutes.

5   While the pastry case is baking, tip the warm cooked pumpkin into a food processor. Add the tofu, spices, sugar, maple syrup, cornflour and salt (if using) and blend to a smooth puree. Pour the filling mixture into the pastry case and bake for 35–40 minutes, or until just set; it should still be slightly wobbly in the middle but will firm up as it cools.

6   Leave the pie to cool on a wire rack. Serve at room temperature or chill in the fridge. Serve with non-dairy cream or vegan ice cream.

BAKER'S TIP

If you prefer, you can use tinned pumpkin puree to make this pie; you'll need a 425g (15oz) tin.

Apricot Bakewell Tart

Named after the Derbyshire town of Bakewell, this tart is traditionally made with a mixture known as frangipane; a blend of ground almonds, eggs, butter and sugar. It is sometimes topped with a glace icing, but here it is finished with fresh apricots, flaked almonds and a dusting of icing sugar.

SERVES 8

For the pastry:
100g/3½oz plain white flour, plus extra for dusting
50g/1¾oz cold unsalted plant butter, diced
25g/1oz ground almonds
25g/1oz icing sugar, sifted
finely grated zest of 1 lemon, preferably unwaxed
1 tsp powdered egg replacer
2 tsp cold water

For the filling:
2 tbsp ground flax seeds (linseed)
6 tbsp cold water
100g/3½oz plant butter or vegan block margarine, softened
150g/5½oz light muscovado or light brown soft sugar
finely grated zest of ½ lemon, preferably unwaxed
½ tsp almond extract
200g/7oz ground almonds
2 tbsp plain white flour
½ tsp baking powder
5 tbsp apricot jam
4 fresh ripe apricots, halved and stones removed
25g/1oz flaked almonds
1 tsp icing sugar, preferably unrefined, to dust

1 To make the pastry, sift the flour into a bowl, add the butter and rub in with your fingertips until the mixture resembles fine breadcrumbs. Stir in the ground almonds, icing sugar and

lemon zest. Mix together the egg replacer and water, add to the dry ingredients and gather together to make a dough.

2 Gently knead the dough on a lightly floured surface for a few seconds until smooth, then form into a ball and flatten slightly (this makes it easier when it comes to rolling out), wrap in cling film (or plastic-free alternative) and chill in the fridge for 10 minutes. Roll out and use to line a loose-bottomed 23cm (9in) fluted flan tin. Chill in the fridge for 10 minutes. Put a baking sheet in the oven and preheat the oven to 190°C/fan oven 170°C/gas 5.

3 Prick the base of the chilled pastry case with a fork and line with non-stick baking paper or foil, pressing it neatly into the corners. Weigh the paper down with dried beans or ceramic baking beans. Put the flan case in the oven on the heated baking sheet. Turn down the temperature to 180°C/fan oven 160°C/gas 4 and bake for 10 minutes, then remove the paper or foil and beans and bake for a further 5 minutes.

4 Meanwhile, make the filling: Mix the ground flax seeds (linseed) and water together in a small bowl and leave for 5 minutes to thicken. Put the plant butter, sugar, lemon zest and almond extract in a bowl and beat together until light and fluffy. Stir in the ground almonds and flax mixture.

5 Sift over the flour and baking powder and gently mix in until combined. Spread the jam over the base of the warm pastry case, then spoon in the filling, levelling the top with the back of the spoon. Press the apricots, cut side up, into the filling at even intervals, then scatter the flaked almonds over the top. Bake for 30–35 minutes, or until the filling is just firm. Dust the top with icing sugar before serving warm or at room temperature.

VARIATION

For a raspberry Bakewell tart, use raspberry jam instead of apricot and use 75g/2¾oz fresh raspberries instead of fresh apricots.

Linzertorte

Named after the Austrian city of Linz, recipes for Linzertorte date back as far as the 1650s. Originally made with a sweet egg-enriched pastry and decorated with an elaborate lattice top, this veganised version is made with an almond-flour pastry and finished with cut-out pastry shapes for a simpler finish.

SERVES 8

1 tsp powdered egg replacer
2–3 tbsp cold water
125g/4¼oz almond flour or ground almonds
175g/6oz plain white flour, plus extra for dusting
2 tbsp caster sugar, preferably golden unrefined
1 tsp ground cinnamon
a pinch of salt
150g/5½oz cold plant butter or vegan block margarine, cubed
300g/10½oz good-quality raspberry jam
plant milk e.g., almond milk, for brushing

1   Whisk the egg replacer with 2 tablespoons of the cold water in a bowl. Put the almond flour or ground almonds, flour, sugar, cinnamon and salt in a bowl and stir together to mix. Add the butter and rub in until the mixture resembles breadcrumbs. Sprinkle over the egg replacer and stir together, adding a little more water if needed to mix to a firm dough.

2   Knead the pastry for a few seconds on a lightly floured surface until smooth. Form into a ball then flatten slightly (this makes it easier when it comes to rolling out), wrap in cling film (or plastic-free alternative) and chill in the fridge for 10 minutes. Put a baking sheet in the oven and preheat to 180°C/fan oven 160°C/gas 4. Roll out three-quarters of the pastry and use to line a 23cm (9in) flan tin. Reserve any trimmings.

3   Prick the base of the pastry case with a fork and line with non-stick baking paper or foil, pressing it neatly into the corners. Weigh the paper down with dried beans or ceramic baking beans. Put the flan case in the oven on the heated baking sheet and bake for 10 minutes, then remove the paper or foil and beans and bake for a further 5 minutes.

4   While the pastry case is baking, roll out the remaining pastry and cut out pastry shapes about 5cm (2 in) in diameter such as stars. Re-roll the trimmings and cut out more shapes. Lightly brush the tops with plant milk. Spoon the jam into the warm pastry case and spread out in an even layer. Arrange the pastry shapes on top.

5   Bake the Linzertorte for 15–20 minutes, or until the pastry shapes are golden and cooked and the jam bubbling. Remove from the oven and leave to cool for at least 5 minutes before cutting and serving; vegan 'crème fraîche' is a great accompaniment.

BAKER'S TIP

An authentic Linzertorte is always made with redcurrant jelly or raspberry jam, but you can use any flavour you like.

Apple and Blueberry Pie

For an easy way to make fruit pie, make an open-topped parcel and cook on a baking tray – there's no pie dish to cover or flan tin to line. As the pastry needs to be fairly flexible to be shaped in this way, it contains vegan egg replacer which enriches it and stops it being too crumbly.

SERVES 6

For the pastry:
100g/3½oz plain white flour
50g/1¾oz plain wholemeal flour
1 tsp ground mixed spice
a pinch of salt (optional)
75g/2¾oz cold plant butter or vegan block margarine, cut into small cubes
25g/1oz icing sugar
1 tsp (3g) powdered egg replacer
1½ tbsp cold water
2 tbsp plant milk e.g., unsweetened soya or oat milk, for brushing

For the filling:
450g/1lb eating apples, such as Cox or Russet
40g/1½oz light muscovado or light brown soft sugar
1 tsp ground cinnamon
100g/3½oz fresh or frozen blueberries

vegan ice cream, vegan yogurt or vegan crème fraiche (e.g., oat fraiche), to serve

1   To make the pastry, sift the flours, spice and salt (if using) into a bowl, adding the bran left in the sieve. Add the butter and rub it in with your fingertips until the mixture resembles fine breadcrumbs. Sift over the icing sugar and stir in.

2 Whisk the egg replacer with the cold water in a bowl and drizzle it over the dry ingredients. Stir to make a soft dough, adding a few more drops of water if necessary. Shape into a ball, flatten slightly (this makes it easier when it comes to rolling out), wrap in cling film (or plastic-free alternative) and chill in the fridge for 20–30 minutes.

3 Preheat the oven to 190°C/fan oven 170°C/gas 5. Line a large baking sheet with non-stick baking paper. Quarter, core, peel and thickly slice the apples and put in a bowl. Sprinkle over half of the sugar and all the cinnamon and mix with your hands to coat all the apple slices evenly. Mix in the blueberries.

4 Roll out the pastry on the lined baking sheet to a 30cm (12in) round. Scatter over half of the remaining sugar. Pile the fruit mixture in the middle of the pastry, then draw up the sides of the pastry over the fruit but not completely, leaving the middle – 12–15cm (4¾–6in) diameter – open and uncovered.

5 Brush the pastry edge with plant milk. Sprinkle the remaining sugar over the top of the fruit. Bake for 30–35 minutes, or until the pastry is golden brown and the apples are lightly browned and tender. Check the pie about 10 minutes before the end of cooking time. If the fruit is browning too much, cover with a circle of foil. (Don't do this at the beginning of cooking as some of the juices from the fruit need to evaporate to prevent the pastry becoming soggy.) Serve warm with vegan ice cream, vegan yogurt or vegan crème fraîche.

Blackcurrant Cheesecake

Silken tofu is an excellent egg replacer especially in cheesecakes and similar bakes where the smooth texture works well. It also provides a good source of both protein and calcium. Rather than a crushed biscuit base, the cheesecake filling is encased in a crisp biscuit-type pastry and topped with a sweet and sharp blackcurrant fruit topping.

SERVES 8-10

For the pastry:
125g/4¼oz plain white flour, plus extra for dusting
25g/1oz caster sugar
70g/2½oz cold plant butter, cut into cubes
1 tbsp cold water

For the filling:
100g/3½oz cashew nuts
100g/3½oz coconut cream
finely grated zest of 1 large lemon, preferably unwaxed, plus
　2 tbsp lemon juice
450g/1lb silken tofu
40g/1½oz caster sugar
30g/1oz cornflour

For the topping:
150g/5½oz fresh or frozen blackcurrants
3 tbsp blackcurrant conserve
4 tbsp caster sugar
1 tsp arrowroot or cornflour
1 tbsp lemon juice

1　The day before you plan to bake the cheesecake, put the cashew nuts for the filling in a heatproof bowl. Pour over enough boiling water to cover and leave to cool. Cover and leave in the fridge for at least 6 hours or overnight, if preferred.

2   To make the pastry, sift the flour into a bowl and stir in the sugar. Add the butter or margarine and rub in with your fingertips until the mixture resembles fine breadcrumbs. Sprinkle over the cold water and mix until everything comes together to form a dough. Gently knead on a lightly floured surface for a few seconds, then form into a ball, flatten slightly (this makes it easier when it comes to rolling out), wrap in cling film (or plastic-free alternative) and chill in the fridge for 10 minutes.

3   Put a baking sheet in the oven and preheat to 200°C/fan oven 180°C/gas 6. Roll out the pastry and use to line a 23cm (9in) loose-bottomed fluted flan tin. Prick the base of the pastry case with a fork and line with non-stick baking paper or foil, pressing it neatly into the corners. Weigh the paper down with dried beans or ceramic baking beans. Put the flan case in the oven on the heated baking sheet and bake for 10 minutes, then remove the paper or foil and beans and bake for a further 5 minutes.

4   Lower the oven temperature to 170°C/fan oven 150°C/gas 3. While the pastry case is cooking, drain the cashew nuts and tip into a food processor. Add the coconut cream, lemon zest and juice and blend until smooth, scraping down the sides halfway through blending. Add the tofu, sugar and cornflour and blend again. Spoon and scrape the mixture into the case, then smooth the top level.

5   Bake for 25–30 minutes, or until lightly set (it should still be very slightly wobbly in the centre but will firm up as it cools). Turn off the oven and leave for 10 minutes, then open the oven and leave the door slightly ajar. Leave the cheesecake until cold.

6   For the topping, put the blackcurrants, conserve and sugar into a small heavy-based saucepan. Blend the arrowroot or cornflour and lemon juice together in a small bowl and add to

the pan. Bring to the boil and simmer for 2–3 minutes until thickened. Leave to cool for a few minutes, then spoon on top of the cheesecake. Leave until cold, then chill in the fridge for at least 1 hour, before serving.

BAKER'S TIP

Allowing the cheesecake to cool slowly in the oven will help prevent the filling cracking. Don't worry if small cracks appear as the topping will cover these.

Mince Pies

Traditional mincemeat is made with beef suet and although you may find a brand made with vegetable suet, suitable for vegans, it is very simple to make from scratch. Feel free to substitute any dried fruit combination you like or have to hand, but keep the quantity the same. The coconut pastry here is unlike traditional pastry and when made will be soft and look a little greasy; it becomes beautifully crisp as it bakes.

MAKES 12

For the vegan mincemeat (makes 350g/12oz):
150g/5½oz dried mixed fruit
50g/1¾oz dried cranberries
1 eating apple, quartered, cored, peeled and finely chopped
finely grated zest and juice of 1 orange, preferably unwaxed
finely grated zest and juice of 1 lemon, preferably unwaxed
50g/1¾oz light muscovado or coconut sugar
½ tsp ground mixed spice
½ tsp ground cinnamon
½ tsp ground ginger
25g/1oz toasted flaked almonds (optional)
5 tbsp brandy, rum, port or sherry (see Baker's Tip)

For the coconut pastry:
250g/9oz plain white flour, plus extra for dusting
a pinch of salt (optional)
125g/4¼oz coconut oil, melted
6 tbsp maple syrup or carob and maple syrup blend
1 tsp vanilla extract
1 tbsp icing sugar

1 To make the mincemeat, put the dried fruit, cranberries, chopped apple, orange and lemon zest and juice, sugar and spices in a saucepan. Bring to the boil, stirring occasionally until the sugar has dissolved, then simmer gently for 15 minutes, or until the apple pieces are really soft. Remove from the heat, stir in the flaked almonds (if using) and the brandy, rum, port or sherry. Spoon into hot sterilised jars and seal, or if you are planning to use straight away, leave to cool. This will keep for up to 4 months in a cool cupboard. Once opened, store in the fridge.

2 To make the pastry, sift the flour and salt (if using) into a bowl. Stir the melted oil, maple syrup and vanilla extract together, then add to the flour and mix together with a fork to make a soft dough; wrap in cling film (or plastic-free alternative) and chill in the fridge for 5 minutes. Cut off slightly less than a quarter of the dough and put it back in the fridge for a further 10 minutes.

3 Divide the rest of the pastry into 12 equal-sized pieces. Shape each into a ball, then, using your thumbs, press into the cups of a 12-hole non-stick cupcake tin, shaping and pressing them out evenly so that they cover the base and come just over halfway up the sides of each hole to make pastry cases. Prick the bases with a fork. Chill in the fridge for 15 minutes.

4 Meanwhile, preheat the oven to 180°C/fan oven 160°C/gas 4. Roll out the reserved pastry on a lightly floured surface to a thickness of about 3mm and cut out twelve shapes (e.g., stars) which will be used to top the mince pies.

5 Bake the pastry cases for 10 minutes until beginning to dry out and colour. Remove from the oven and add a generous heaped tablespoon of mincemeat to each pastry case. Top with a pastry shape, return to the oven and bake for a further 10 minutes, or until the pastry is lightly browned and crisp.

Remove from the oven and leave to stand for 5 minutes, then carefully remove the pies. Generously dust with icing sugar and serve warm or cold.

BAKER'S TIP

If you prefer a non-alcoholic mincemeat, use apple juice instead of the alcohol, store the mincemeat in the fridge and use within 1 month of making.

Lemon Meringue Pie

The traditional lemon meringue pie is heavily reliant on eggs to make both the lemon curd filling and the meringue topping but it's not impossible to make a delicious vegan version. This one has a rich nutty pastry, a 'buttery' lemon curd filling and an airy meringue topping made with aquafaba.

SERVES 8

For the pastry:
100g/3½oz plant butter or vegan block margarine, softened
1½ tbsp smooth hazelnut or cashew nut butter
175g/6oz plain white flour, plus extra for dusting
2 tbsp cold water

For the lemon filling:
45g/1½oz cornflour
a small pinch of ground turmeric
5 tbsp cold water
150ml/¼ pint plant milk e.g., rice, almond or oat milk
finely grated zest of 2 lemons, preferably unwaxed, plus
    150ml/¼ pint lemon juice
175g/6oz caster sugar, preferably golden unrefined
a pinch of salt
10g/⅓oz plant butter

For the meringue topping:
5 tbsp aquafaba (page 13)
a pinch of cream of tartar
100g/3½oz caster sugar
½ tsp vanilla extract

1   To make the pastry, blend the plant butter with the nut butter in a bowl until mixed. Scoop out onto a piece of baking paper and chill in the freezer for 10 minutes. Sift the flour into the

bowl, then add the butter and nut butter blend, cut into small pieces, and rub in with your fingertips until the mixture resembles fine breadcrumbs. Stir in enough of the cold water to make a dough.

2 Gently knead the dough on a lightly floured surface until smooth to make a ball, then flatten slightly (this makes it easier when it comes to rolling out), wrap in cling film (or plastic-free alternative) and chill in the fridge for 10 minutes. Put a baking sheet in the oven and preheat to 190°C/fan oven 170°C/gas 5.

3 Roll out the pastry and use to line a 23cm (9in) loose-bottomed fluted flan tin. Prick the base of the pastry case with a fork and line with non-stick baking paper or foil, pressing it neatly into the corners. Weigh the paper down with dried beans or ceramic baking beans. Put the flan case in the oven on the heated baking sheet. Turn down the temperature to 180°C/fan oven 160°C/gas 4 and bake for 10 minutes, then remove the paper or foil and beans and bake for a further 5 minutes.

4 While the pastry is baking, make the lemon filling. Put the cornflour and turmeric in a heavy-based saucepan and add the water. Mix to a paste, then stir in the milk, lemon zest, juice, sugar and salt. Place over a medium heat and bring to the boil, stirring all the time. Simmer for 2–3 minutes, or until thickened.

5 Remove the pan from the heat and stir in the butter. Cover with a piece of wet greaseproof paper (this prevents a skin from forming) and leave until barely warm. Stir the filling, then spoon into the pastry case, spreading evenly.

6 Put the aquafaba and cream of tartar in a bowl and whisk with a hand-held whisk on the highest setting for 2–3 minutes, or until thick and foamy. Gradually add the sugar, a spoonful at a

time, whisking well after each addition, until thick and glossy and stiff peaks form when the whisk is lifted. Add the vanilla extract with the last spoonful of sugar.

7 Preheat the grill to high. Spoon the meringue over the filling, right up to the edges of the pastry case. Place under the grill and rotate frequently, until the meringue is a dark golden brown, watching all the time to make sure that it doesn't burn. Alternatively, brown the top with a kitchen blowtorch. Serve straight away if possible. Alternatively, keep in the fridge until ready to serve; the meringue may fall a little, but should keep for up to 24 hours.

VARIATION

For a lime meringue pie, substitute limes and lime juice for the lemons and lemon juice.

CHAPTER FIVE

Breads and Scones

The benefits of home-baked bread are obvious; you know exactly what's in it. This is particularly important for vegans, as not all commercial breads are suitable and may contain dairy ingredients such as whey or non-vegan stabilisers. Another advantage of making your own bread is that you can adjust flavourings to suit your personal preferences and can be sure that there are no additives or preservatives; it can be very rewarding and there's nothing quite like the flavour and aroma of a freshly baked loaf.

If you don't have time to knead dough and wait for it to rise, there are plenty of alternatives here, such as Courgette Soda Bread and Cornbread. Of course, there's more to bread than just sliced as sandwiches or toast or as an accompaniment to a meal; it can be the star of the show. You might like to try the Roasted Vegetable Stromboli or Mushroom and Crème Fraîche Pizzas.

For those who love sweet bakes, try Cinnamon and Pecan Buns or a spectacular star-shaped Pandoro to serve at Christmas. You'll also find recipes for scones here; both traditional plain ones to serve with whipped coconut cream and jam for a traditional 'cream' tea or savoury treats such as the 'Cheese' and Watercress Scones. Try serving some of these bakes to your non-vegan friends; they are bound to ask you for the recipes.

Vegan Loaf

Vegans need to make sure they get certain nutrients, including vitamins B12 and D, calcium, iodine and omega-3s which are usually obtained from meat, fish and dairy. If you eat bread daily, it's worth making a loaf that suits your needs rather than taking daily supplements. Make sure you choose fortified plant milk (containing additional B12, vitamin D and calcium).

MAKES 1 LOAF (ABOUT 750G/1LB 10OZ)

250g/9oz strong white bread flour, plus extra for dusting
250g/9oz strong wholemeal bread flour
1¼ tsp iodised salt
2 tsp light muscovado or light brown soft sugar
1 tbsp ground flax seeds (linseed)
1 tbsp each of pumpkin seeds, sunflower seeds and sesame seeds
50g/1¾oz Brazil nuts, finely chopped
1½ tsp fast-action dried yeast
325ml/11fl oz plant milk (e.g., unsweetened soya milk or oat milk), plus extra for glazing
2 tbsp rapeseed oil

1   Sift the flours and salt into a mixing bowl, adding the bran left in the sieve. Stir in the sugar, ground flax seeds (linseed), seeds, nuts and yeast. Make a hollow in the middle of the dry ingredients.
2   Add the plant milk and oil and mix to a soft dough. Turn out onto a lightly floured surface and knead for 7–8 minutes, or until the dough is smooth and elastic.
3   Place the dough in a lightly oiled bowl and cover with oiled cling film (or plastic-free alternative) or a damp clean tea towel. Leave to rise in a warm place for 1 hour, or until doubled in size.

4 Grease a 900g (2lb) loaf tin and line the base with a rectangle of non-stick baking paper. Knock back the dough and shape it into a log, then place in the tin. Cover with cling film and leave to rise somewhere warm for about 25 minutes, or until the dough reaches the top of the tin.

5 About 10 minutes before the end of proving time, preheat the oven to 220°C/fan oven 200°C/gas 7. Remove the cling film and brush the top of the loaf with plant milk. Put the loaf in the oven, then turn down the temperature to 200°C/fan oven 180°C/gas 6.

6 Bake for about 35 minutes, or until the loaf sounds hollow when removed from the tin and tapped underneath. Cool on a wire rack.

BAKER'S TIP

You can also make this bread in a bread machine; check your manual to see whether the dry ingredients or liquid ones should be added first (this will depend on the model). Cook on a basic white bread setting.

Courgette Soda Bread

When you don't have the time or patience to make a yeasted bread, this is a quick alternative as there's no need for long kneading and waiting for the dough to rise. It doesn't contain a huge amount of courgette, just enough to add moistness and give the loaf a lovely speckled appearance.

MAKES 1 LOAF (ABOUT 450G/1LB)

2 tsp lemon juice
175ml/6fl oz plant milk e.g., unsweetened oat or soya milk
150g/5½oz self-raising wholemeal flour, plus extra for
   dusting
150g/5½oz plain white flour
1 tsp baking powder
1 tsp bicarbonate of soda
1 tsp salt
freshly ground black pepper
1 medium courgette (about 150g/5½oz), coarsely grated
3 tbsp toasted mixed seeds e.g., pumpkin, sunflower and
   sesame seeds

1 Stir the lemon juice into the plant milk and leave at room temperature for a few minutes while preparing the remaining ingredients. Preheat the oven to 200°C/fan oven 180°C/gas 6. Lightly grease a baking sheet or line it with non-stick baking paper.

2 Sift the flours, baking powder, bicarbonate of soda, salt and a pinch of pepper into a mixing bowl, adding the bran left in the sieve. Stir in the grated courgette and seeds and make a hollow in the middle of the ingredients. Add the vegan buttermilk and mix together, taking care not to overmix.

3 Turn out the dough onto a lightly floured work surface and shape into a round about 18cm (7in) in diameter. Transfer to

the prepared baking sheet. Lightly dust the top with flour, then cut a deep cross on the top, cutting almost through to the base of the loaf.

4 Bake for 30 minutes, or until well risen and browned and the loaf sounds hollow when you tap the bottom. Transfer to a wire rack and leave for at least 20 minutes before slicing or tearing into portions. Serve warm or cold.

BAKER'S TIP

Soda bread relies on the acidity of the vegan 'buttermilk' – plant milk and lemon juice – to boost the rise and give it an airy texture, so make sure you allow this to stand for at least 5 minutes at room temperature before using. The milk will thicken and curdle slightly during this time.

Cornbread

An American classic, freshly baked cornbread is a great accompaniment to vegan soups, stews and dishes like chilli. Usually containing eggs and dairy buttermilk, this egg-free version is easy to make and quick to bake and relies on bicarbonate of soda, a dash of vinegar and fizzy water to aerate the mixture and create a light spongy texture.

MAKES 9 SQUARES

200g/7oz fine polenta or fine cornmeal, plus 1 tbsp for sprinkling
200g/7oz plain white flour
3/4 tsp salt
1 tsp baking powder
1/2 tsp bicarbonate of soda
2 tbsp nutritional yeast (optional)
450ml/1 pint plant milk e.g., unsweetened soya or oat milk
2 tbsp rapeseed oil or sunflower oil
1 tbsp cider vinegar
2 tbsp maple or agave syrup
5 tbsp sparkling water

1   Preheat the oven to 180°C/fan oven 160°C/gas 4. Lightly grease a 23cm (9in) square cake tin and line the base with non-stick baking paper.
2   Put the 200g/7oz polenta or cornmeal in a bowl. Sift over the flour, salt, baking powder and bicarbonate of soda. Add the nutritional yeast (if using) then stir the dry ingredients together and make a hollow in the middle. Mix the plant milk, oil, vinegar and syrup together in a jug. Add the sparkling water and pour into the hollow.
3   Stir everything together until just combined; do not overmix, it should still look very lumpy. Pour and scrape the mixture

into the prepared tin and level the top with the back of a spoon. Sprinkle the remaining tablespoon of polenta or cornmeal evenly over the top.

4   Bake for 25 minutes, or until the top is until golden brown and the cornbread is just starting to shrink away at the edges of the tin. Put the tin on a wire rack and leave to cool before turning out and cutting into squares. Store in an airtight tin or container and eat within 4 days of making.

VARIATIONS

For cheese and onion cornbread, stir 30g/1oz finely grated vegan Parmesan and 4 very thinly sliced spring onions into the dry ingredients.

For chilli cornbread, halve, deseed and finely chop 1 red and 1 green chilli and stir in with the milk mixture.

Honeycomb Bread

These Middle Eastern tear-and-share sweet buns are known as 'khaliat nahal', meaning 'beehive', as they fit together like honeycomb hexagons. They are usually filled with a soft curd or cream cheese, scattered with black sesame seeds and drizzled with honey. This, of course, is a vegan bee-friendly version drizzled with sugar syrup – or you could use dandelion 'honey' instead (page 81).

MAKES 16 SMALL ROLLS

450g/1lb strong white bread flour, plus extra for dusting
1 tsp salt
100g/3½oz caster sugar
7g/¼oz sachet fast-action dried yeast
50g/1¾oz plant butter or vegan margarine
150ml/¼ pint near-boiling water
150ml/¼ pint plant milk e.g., unsweetened soya or oat milk
100g/3½oz full-fat vegan cream cheese alternative
2 tsp sesame seeds, preferably black

1   Lightly grease a 24cm (9½in) round cake tin and line the base with a circle of non-stick baking paper. Sift the flour and salt into a bowl. Stir in 1 tablespoon of the sugar, then the yeast. Put the butter in a heatproof jug with the near-boiling water and leave until the butter has melted. Stir in the plant milk. Reserve 1 tablespoon of the mixture for glazing the rolls later, then pour most of the remaining milk and butter into the dry ingredients and mix to form a soft dough, adding a little more if the dough is a little dry. Knead the dough on a lightly floured surface for 7–8 minutes until smooth and elastic. Cover the dough with the upturned bowl and allow it to rest for 10 minutes.

2   Divide the dough into 16 equal-sized pieces. Flatten one piece into a disc in the palm of your hand, then put about ½ teaspoon

of the vegan cream cheese in the middle. Draw up the edges around the cheese and pinch together to enclose it, then gently roll into a ball. Repeat with the rest of the dough balls and cream cheese.

3   Arrange the balls of dough in the tin in concentric circles, seam-side down. Cover with a piece of oiled cling film (or plastic-free alternative) and leave in a warm place to rise for about 40 minutes, or until doubled in size. Towards the end of rising time, preheat the oven to 200°C/fan oven 180°C/gas 6.

4   Remove the cling film and brush the tops with the reserved milk mixture and scatter with the sesame seeds. Bake for 25–30 minutes, or until golden brown.

5   While the buns are baking, put the rest of the sugar in a saucepan with 5 tablespoons of cold water. Slowly bring to the boil, stirring until the sugar has dissolved. Simmer for 3–4 minutes until slightly reduced and syrupy. Remove the syrup from the heat and leave to cool for 5–10 minutes.

6   Take the buns out of the oven and place the tin on a wire rack. Let them cool for 4–5 minutes, then slowly drizzle the syrup over the tops of the warm buns, letting it soak in before pouring on more. Let them cool for 15 minutes before turning out of the tin and serving warm.

BAKER'S TIP

Black sesame seeds have a much nuttier flavour than white sesame seeds and are slightly bitter, which works well with the sweetness of the bread. Use whichever you prefer for these buns.

Pandoro

The sister cake of fruited panettone, pandoro is a traditional Christmas treat form the northern Italian town of Verona which is finished with a snow-like dusting of icing sugar. It can be baked in a round tin, but for the classic star-shaped sweet bread, use a star-shaped pandoro tin.

MAKES 1

500g/1lb 2oz strong white flour, plus extra for dusting
1 tsp salt
125g/4¼oz caster sugar
10g/⅓oz fast-action dried yeast
finely grated zest of 1 orange, preferably unwaxed
finely grated zest of 1 lemon, preferably unwaxed
150g/5½oz unsalted plant butter, softened, plus extra for greasing
140ml/4¾fl oz aquafaba (page 13)
2 tsp vanilla extract
100ml/3½fl oz warm plant milk e.g., unsweetened almond or soya milk
icing sugar, for dusting

1 Put the flour in a bread machine or in a stand mixer fitted with a dough hook. Add the salt and sugar on one side of the bread machine pan or mixer bowl and the yeast on the other side. Add the orange and lemon zest, plant butter, aquafaba and vanilla extract. Pour in the milk.

2 If using a bread machine, set to the dough setting and press 'start'. If using a stand mixer, start on a slow speed and mix to form a soft sticky dough, then increase to a higher speed and mix for 10 minutes.

3 Turn out the dough onto a lightly floured work surface, shape into a ball with floured hands (it will still be sticky) and place in a lightly greased bowl. Cover with cling film (or plastic-free

alternative) and leave to prove somewhere warm until doubled in size; this can take up to 3 hours in a warm place, or you can leave it somewhere cool overnight.

4   Grease a 20cm (8in) diameter x 15cm (16in) high pandoro tin with softened unsalted plant butter. Tip the dough out onto a lightly floured work surface and knead to knock out all the air. Shape the dough into a ball and put it into the prepared tin, pressing it flat into the corners. Cover with oiled cling film and leave to rise somewhere warm until the dough comes just a few millimetres below the top of the tin; this will take 1½–2 hours.

5   When the dough is almost ready, preheat the oven to 190°C/fan oven 170°C/gas 5. Remove the cling film and bake the pandoro for 35–40 minutes, or until a skewer inserted into the middle comes out clean.

6   Remove from the oven and cover with a clean tea towel. Leave to cool in the tin for 5 minutes, then – making sure the edges are loose – turn out onto a wire rack. Cover with the tea towel to keep it moist and leave to cool. Trim the base with a serrated knife so that the pandoro will sit flat on a plate. To serve pandoro, cut into horizontal slices; ones at the top should be thicker and those at the base slightly thinner so that the portions are fairly equal. Rearrange the pandoro in its original shape and dust generously with icing sugar.

BAKER'S TIP

Bread machines differ, so check the instructions for yours; you may need to put the milk in the pan first, then add the dry ingredients.

Cinnamon and Pecan Buns

These sticky nut and spice buns are made with a soft sweet bread dough enriched with vegan yogurt and vegan cream cheese. Baking the buns together in a tin, rather than separately, keeps the sides of the buns beautifully soft.

MAKES 9

300g/10½oz plain white flour, plus extra for dusting
2 tsp baking powder
¼ tsp bicarbonate of soda
¼ tsp salt
50g/1¾oz plant butter or vegan block margarine
40g/1½oz caster sugar
150g/5½oz full-fat vegan cream cheese alternative
3 tbsp vegan yogurt e.g., coconut or soya yogurt
1–2 tbsp plant milk e.g., unsweetened soya or oat milk
2 tbsp maple or agave syrup, for brushing

For the filling:
50g/1¾oz plant butter or vegan block margarine, softened
50g/1¾oz light muscovado or light brown soft sugar
2 tsp ground cinnamon
75g/2¾oz pecan pieces, roughly chopped

1   Preheat the oven to 200°C/fan oven 180°C/gas 6. Grease a 25 x 20cm (10 x 8in) traybake or rectangular tin and line the base with baking parchment.

2   For the filling, mix together the plant butter or margarine, muscovado sugar and cinnamon together in a bowl and set aside.

3   Sift the flour, baking powder, bicarbonate of soda and salt into a mixing bowl. Add the plant butter or margarine and rub in with your fingertips until the mixture resembles fine breadcrumbs. Stir in the sugar.

4   Mix the vegan cream cheese, yogurt and 1 tablespoon of the milk together in a bowl. Add the dry ingredients and mix to form a soft dough, adding a little more of the milk if needed. Roll out on a lightly floured surface to a square about 25cm (10in).

5   Spread the butter, sugar and cinnamon mixture over the dough as evenly as possible, then scatter with the chopped pecan pieces. Roll up the dough to resemble a Swiss roll. Using a sharp knife, cut the roll into 9 even-sized pieces. Arrange the buns, cut side up, in the prepared tin in 3 rows of 3, setting them slightly apart.

6   Bake for 20–25 minutes until dark golden brown. Remove the tin from the oven and place on a wire rack. Leave for 5 minutes, then carefully remove the buns from the tin. Brush the tops with the maple or agave syrup while still warm. They are best eaten on the day of making.

VARIATION

For ginger and walnut buns, substitute ground ginger for the cinnamon and walnuts for the pecans.

Roasted Vegetable Stromboli

This filled bread, somewhat like a rolled-up pizza, is usually filled with sliced meats such as salami or prosciutto, and dairy cheese. This one contains ready-prepared roasted vegetables and meltingly soft vegan mozzarella.

SERVES 4-6

450g/1lb strong white bread flour, plus extra for dusting
50g/1¾oz chickpea flour or besan (gram) flour
1 tsp salt
50g/1¾oz fine polenta or fine cornmeal, plus extra for dusting
7g/¼oz sachet easy-blend dried yeast
2 tbsp olive oil
320ml/11fl oz warm water

For the filling:
250-300g/9-10½oz jar roasted red peppers, drained
250-300g/9-10½oz jar sun-dried tomatoes in oil, drained (reserve the oil)
1 tsp dried mixed herbs
grated zest of 1 lemon, preferably unwaxed, plus 1 tsp lemon juice
8 pitted black olives, quartered
140-150g/5-5½oz jar chargrilled artichokes, drained
150g/5½oz vegan mozzarella alternative
30g/1oz fresh basil leaves, large ones torn into small pieces
freshly ground black pepper

1   To make the dough, sift the bread flour, chickpea flour and salt into a mixing bowl. Stir in the cornmeal and yeast and make a hollow in the middle. Add the olive oil and water and mix to form a soft dough. Turn out onto a lightly floured surface and knead for 5-6 minutes until smooth and springy. Put into a

clean bowl, cover with cling film (or plastic-free alternative) or a clean tea towel and leave in a warm place for about 1 hour, or until doubled in size. Cut a piece of non-stick baking paper to fit a large baking sheet.

2   Meanwhile, make the filling. Put half the peppers, half the sun-dried tomatoes, herbs, lemon zest and black pepper in a food processor. Add 2 tablespoons of oil, reserved from the sun-dried tomatoes, and the lemon juice, then blend until fairly smooth. Spoon into a bowl and stir in the olives.

3   Thinly slice the remaining roasted red peppers, sun-dried tomatoes and artichokes. Coarsely grate the vegan cheese or cut into small cubes.

4   Turn out the dough and knock out it back with your knuckles to deflate. Roll out to a rectangle roughly 45 x 30cm (18 x 12in); the dough will be very springy, so don't worry if your rectangle has quite wavy edges. Spread the red pepper and tomato paste over the dough to within 1cm (½in) of the edges. Top with the sliced red peppers, tomatoes and artichokes, then scatter over the basil and cheese.

5   Fold over the two shorter ends of the dough by about 3cm (1¼in), then roll up from a long side. Scatter the lined baking sheet with polenta or cornmeal, then place the stromboli on top, seam-side down. Cover with oiled cling film (or plastic-free alternative) and leave in a warm place to rise for 30–40 minutes. About 10 minutes before the end of rising time, preheat the oven to 200°C/fan oven 180°C/gas 6.

6   Bake the stromboli for 30 minutes, or until well risen and dark golden brown. Remove from the oven and leave for 5 minutes. Serve warm or leave to cool completely. Cut into thick slices.

BAKER'S TIPS

The stromboli is good warm, but is best cold the next day when the dough will have softened a little and soaked up the flavours. If serving cold, wrap in cling film (or plastic-free alternative) or tightly in foil as soon as it is cool. It will be fine at room temperature for up to 24 hours, but store in the fridge if the weather is very warm.

Chickpea flour or besan (gram) flour is a useful addition to the bread dough. Although it is gluten-free (so can't be used in large quantities for bread-making), it has a high protein content (more than double the amount of wheat flours).

Mushroom and Crème Fraîche Pizzas

Vegan crème fraîche alternative and vegan parmesan make a lovely cheesy topping for these pizzas. Dried porcini mushrooms have an intense flavour which works well here.

SERVES 2

For the pizza base:
175g/6oz strong white bread flour, plus extra for dusting
50g/1¾oz wholemeal or brown bread flour
¼ tsp salt
1 tsp dried mixed herbs
1 tsp easy-blend dried yeast
3 tbsp nutritional yeast (optional)
150ml/¼ pint warm water
1 tbsp olive oil

For the mushroom topping:
15g/½oz dried porcini mushrooms
3 tbsp olive oil
300g/10½oz mixed fresh mushrooms or chestnut mushrooms, sliced
1–2 garlic cloves, peeled and crushed (optional)
1 tbsp chopped fresh sage
200g/7oz tub vegan crème fraîche alternative e.g., oat fraîche
40g/1½oz vegan parmesan, grated
2 handfuls of fresh rocket leaves
freshly ground black pepper

1   For the base, sift the flours and salt into a bowl, adding the bran left in the sieve. Stir in the herbs, dried yeast and nutritional yeast (if using). Add the water and oil and mix to form a soft dough. Turn out the dough onto a lightly floured surface and knead for 8–10 minutes until smooth and elastic. Put the dough into a clean bowl, cover with cling film or a tea towel and leave in a warm place for about an hour, or until doubled in size.

2   While the dough is rising, make the topping. Put the porcini mushrooms in a small heatproof bowl and pour over boiling water to cover. Leave to soak for 20 minutes, then drain, rinse, pat dry on kitchen paper and roughly chop. Heat the oil in a frying pan over a medium heat, add the sliced mushrooms and the porcini mushrooms, and stir-fry for 2 minutes, then add the garlic (if using) and the sage. Cook for a further minute or two until softened. Turn off the heat. Season with freshly ground black pepper.

3   Put two baking sheets in the oven, then preheat the oven to 220°C/fan oven 200°C/gas 7. Knock back the pizza dough and divide it in half. Roll out each piece on a lightly floured surface to a circle 22–25cm (8½–10in), depending on your preferred thickness of pizza.

4   Carefully slide the pizzas onto the hot baking sheets and top with the mushrooms, crème fraîche alternative and a scattering of grated vegan parmesan, dividing everything equally between the two bases. Bake for 14–15 minutes, or until the bases are cooked through and the topping is golden-brown. Leave to cool for 2 minutes, and before serving, scatter a handful of rocket over the top of each.

BAKER'S TIP

If preferred, use 15g/½oz fresh yeast instead of easy-blend dried yeast. Mix with 3 tablespoons of the flour, a pinch of caster sugar and the warm water. Leave in a warm place for about 15 minutes until frothy before using.

Simple Scones

Traditional scone recipes use butter and milk, but you can use vegan alternatives instead. Dairy-free 'buttermilk' makes the scones extra light, and using oil instead of butter reduces the preparation time and makes the scones a touch healthier too.

MAKES 8

150ml/¼ pint plant milk e.g., unsweetened soya or oat milk, plus extra for brushing

1 tsp lemon juice or cider vinegar

225g/8oz plain white flour, plus extra for dusting

1 tbsp baking powder

a pinch of salt (optional)

1 tbsp caster sugar

5 tbsp rapeseed oil or sunflower oil

vegan 'clotted cream' (see below) or whipped coconut cream (page 21) and jam, to serve

1   Pour the plant milk into a jug and stir in the lemon juice or vinegar. Leave to stand at room temperature for at least 5 minutes; the mixture will thicken and curdle slightly to make a dairy-free buttermilk alternative.

2   Preheat the oven to 220°C/fan oven 200°C/gas 7. Line a baking sheet with non-stick baking paper. Sift the flour, baking powder and salt (if using) into a bowl. Stir in the caster sugar. Drizzle the oil over the flour and stir with a fork until mixed, then add the 'buttermilk' and mix to a stiff dough.

3   Gently knead on a lightly floured surface, then roll out to a thickness of 2cm (¾in) and stamp out 6cm (2½in) rounds with a plain or fluted cutter. Squeeze together the trimmings, re-roll and stamp out more scones. You should have 8 scones in total.

4   Put the scones on the lined baking sheet, spacing them slightly apart to allow room for spreading, then brush the tops

with plant milk. Dust with a little plain flour. Bake for 12–15 minutes, or until well risen and golden brown on both the tops and bases.

5   Cool on a wire rack. Serve slightly warm or cold, split in half and topped with whipped coconut cream and jam, or dairy-free spread if preferred.

BAKER'S TIPS

Instead of stamping out rounds, roll the scone mixture into a 2cm- (¾in-) thick circle and cut into 8 wedges. Separate the triangles and arrange on the baking sheet, spacing slightly apart.

To make vegan 'clotted cream', using a hand-held electric whisk or stand mixer, cream 75g/2¾oz softened vegan butter with 2 tablespoons of sifted icing sugar until pale and fluffy. Add 150ml/¼ pint dairy-free double cream (such as plant cream) and continue to whisk for about 2 minutes until stiff peaks form.

VARIATIONS

For lemon and raisin scones, add the finely grated zest of 1 lemon (preferably unwaxed) and 75g/2¾oz sultanas to the flour mixture.

For wholewheat scone fingers, use 115g/4oz each of plain white and wholewheat flour. Shape the mixture into fingers, rather than rounds, and brush the tops with plant milk and sprinkle with 25g/1oz wheat flakes.

'Cheese' and Watercress Scones

Vegan 'mature Cheddar' is excellent in these light savoury scones. Oats help to bind the mixture together and peppery watercress is a great addition too, as it adds both flavour and moisture, which helps the scones to rise.

MAKES 8 SCONES

150g/5½oz self-raising white flour, plus extra for dusting
150g/5½oz self-raising wholemeal flour
1 tsp baking powder
½ tsp English mustard powder (optional)
50g/1¾oz cold plant butter or vegan block margarine, cut into small cubes
50g/1¾oz rolled (porridge) oats
75g/2¾oz watercress, coarse stalks removed, finely chopped
75g/2¾oz vegan 'mature Cheddar' cheese, grated
100ml/4fl oz plant milk e.g., unsweetened soya or oat milk, plus extra to glaze
salt and freshly ground black pepper

1 Preheat the oven to 220°C/fan oven 200°C/gas 7. Lightly grease a heavy baking sheet or line with non-stick baking paper.
2 Sift the flours, baking powder and mustard powder (if using) into a mixing bowl, then tip in the bran left in the sieve. Season with a little salt and pepper. Add the plant butter or vegan margarine and rub it in with your fingertips until the mixture resembles fine breadcrumbs.
3 Stir in the oats, then stir in the watercress, followed by about three-quarters of the grated cheese. Stir in the milk with a fork to make a very soft dough. Shape into a ball and turn out onto a lightly floured work surface.
4 Roll out the dough to a thickness of about 2cm (¾in). Using a 7.5cm (3in) round cutter, stamp out as many scones as

possible. Gather the trimmings together and re-roll to make the last one or two – you should have about 8 scones. Place on the baking sheet, spacing slightly apart.

5   Lightly brush the tops with plant milk, then sprinkle with the remaining cheese. Bake for 10–14 minutes, or until well risen and golden brown. Transfer to a wire rack to cool and serve barely warm or cool. When cold, store in an airtight container; they are best eaten on the day of making but will keep for a day or two.

BAKER'S TIP

To make triangular scones (or if you don't have a cutter), shape the dough into a round about 2cm (¾in) thick and transfer to the baking sheet. Cut into 8 wedges with a sharp knife, leaving them in place (don't separate). Lightly brush the top with plant milk and sprinkle with the remaining cheese. Bake for 14–15 minutes, or until well risen and golden brown. After baking, cover with a clean tea towel to keep the scones moist.

Index

BAKING IT VEGAN